YOU CAN PAINT

Watercolors

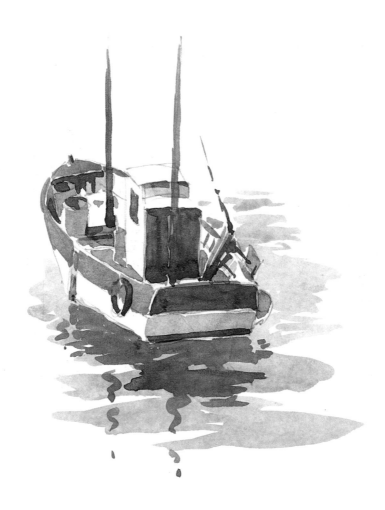

An inspiration to millions of amateur painters,
ALWYN CRAWSHAW has made seven popular TV series on
painting that have been shown worldwide. He is the author
of twenty books on art instruction and teaches popular
workshops and courses. He is a also a regular contributor
to *Leisure Painter* magazine; Founder and President of the
Society of Amateur Artists; President of the National
Acrylic Painters Association; and a member of the Society
of Equestrian Artists and the British Watercolour Society.

YOU CAN PAINT

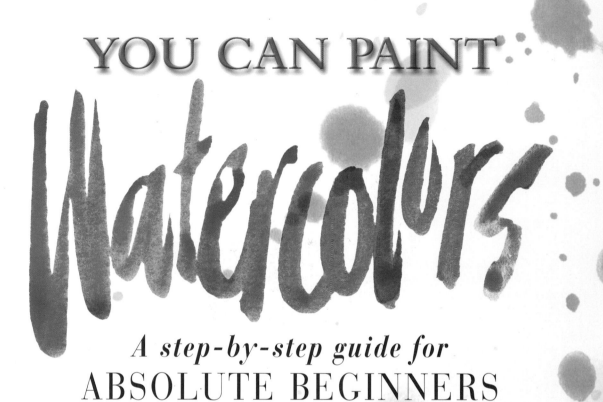

Watercolors

A step-by-step guide for
ABSOLUTE BEGINNERS

ALWYN CRAWSHAW

Watson-Guptill Publications/New York

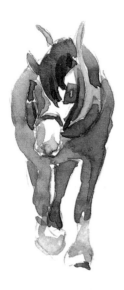

First published in the United States in 2000 by
Watson-Guptill Publications,
a division of BPI Communications, Inc.,
770 Broadway, New York, NY 10003
www.watsonguptill.com

Library of Congress Card Number: 00-104483

ISBN 0-8230-5989-8

First published in the United Kingdom in 2000 by
HarperCollins*Publishers*
77-85 Fulham Palace Road
Hammersmith
London W6 8JB

Editorial Director: Cathy Gosling
Editor: Isobel Smales
Designer: Penny Dawes
Photography: Nigel Cheffers-Heard

Color reproduction by Colourscan, Singapore
Printed and bound by Rotolito Lombarda SpA, Italy

1 2 3 4 5 6 7 / 06 05 04 03 02 01 00

CONTENTS

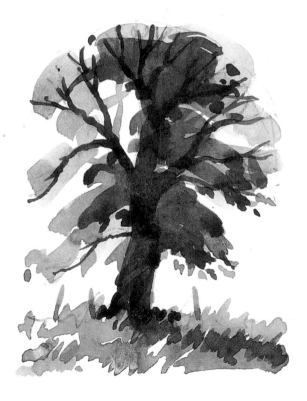

INTRODUCTION

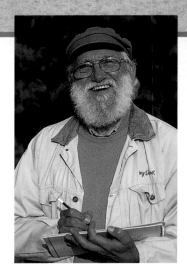

"I can't paint; I'm not an artist." People frequently say this to me, and I always reply, "Have you tried?" Usually the answer is "No," or "Yes, I have tried, but I'm no good." I then ask, "But have you been taught how to paint?" and the answer is always "No." Well, painting is just like any other art or trade: you have to learn in order to progress. You do not expect to be able to play the piano without taking lessons, and so it is with painting. I have been teaching painting for over thirty-five years, and have drawn on all my experience to write this book, which will introduce you to the wonderful world of watercolor painting.

Watercolor is a very popular medium that lends itself to painting a wide range of subjects.

It also has the great advantage that it requires no complicated equipment, which makes it ideal for a beginner. Even when you are painting outdoors, your basic essentials are a pencil, a box of paints, a brush, paper, and water.

The aim of this book is to get you started and then to inspire you to greater heights,

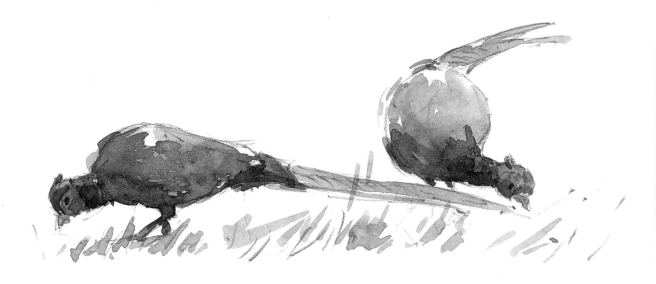

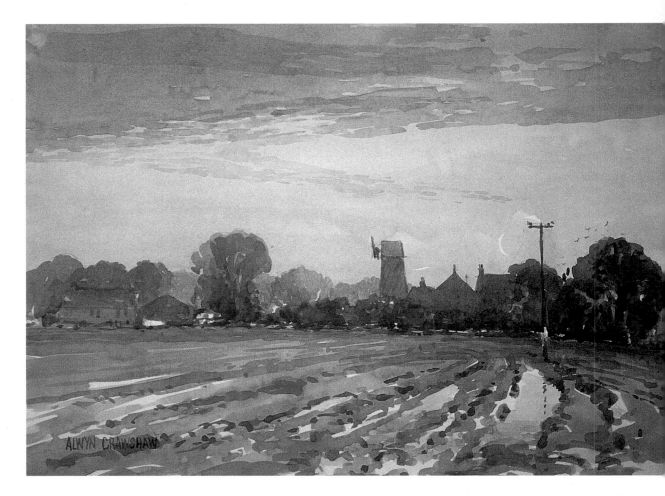

Towards My Studio drawing paper, 11 x 16 in

so I have kept the instructions very simple. I describe all the materials you will need to begin and show you enough basic, traditional watercolor techniques to give you a good grounding. It is very important to practice these basic techniques before you try any "proper" paintings. Don't let your enthusiasm lead you to rush through the book before you have mastered the basics!

Learning can be challenging and rewarding, and is just as enjoyable as producing a masterpiece. Every time you mix a color or paint a brush stroke you will learn a little

more and gain experience. The more experience you have, the more confident you will be and the more you will want to paint. If you follow the book carefully and practice the exercises with a feeling of excitement and enthusiasm, you will be well on your way to becoming a watercolor artist. Above all, it is important to enjoy your painting.

HOW TO USE THIS BOOK

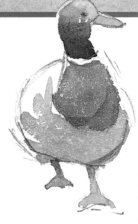

This is an instruction book for absolute beginners. It describes the materials you will need, then shows you the basic watercolor techniques and teaches you simple color mixing. There are exercises and demonstrations for you to copy using the techniques you have learned. I have kept the instructional text short and simple, and the exercises and demonstrations are broken down into simple stages that are easy to follow.

I recommend that you begin by reading the book through without lifting a pencil or a

***Hickling Church** drawing paper, 11 x 16 in*

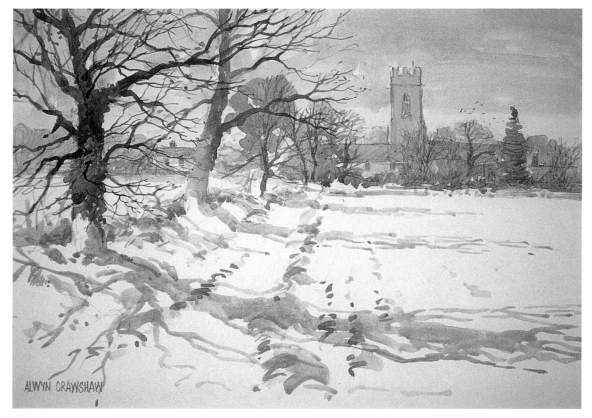

ALWYN CRAWSHAW

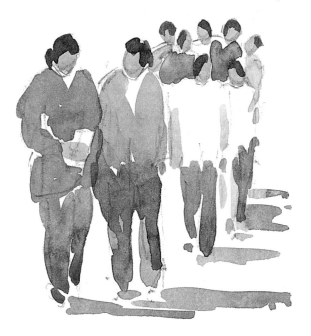

paintbrush. It will be worth the time you spend! Familiarize yourself with the names of the colors and study the techniques to see what each achieves and how it is achieved. Look at the way the paintings progress in the exercises and demonstrations. Once you've read it through, start playing with your materials. Get some inexpensive paper and doodle with your brushes and paints. See what happens when you add water, when you add wet paint onto wet paint, and when you try to paint a thin line. Figure out how long the paint takes to dry. Make friends with your brushes and the paper before you even try color mixing or the different techniques.

When you come to try the demonstrations, you may think that the finished picture is

complicated. But remember, it is the end result of a number of simpler stages. If you follow these stages carefully, step by step, you will see how your painting develops. The size I painted each demonstration painting is shown under its finished stage. Most of the other exercises in the book were painted the same size that they are reproduced.

I am sure that by the time you have reached the end of the book, you will be inspired to try painting some of your own favorite subjects.

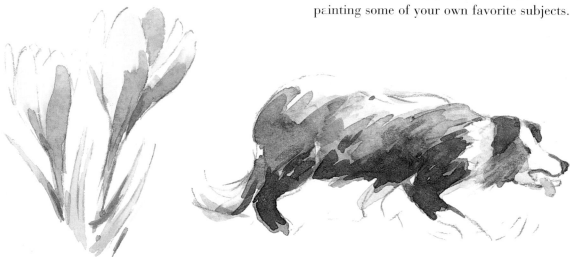

BASIC MATERIALS

As a beginner, you do not need to buy a whole range of expensive art materials. The fewer you have, the fewer you have to master. As you gain experience, you will want to change or extend your range of brushes, paper, colors, etc. It is good to want to progress and experiment, and watercolor is a wonderful medium for exploring. But at the beginning, let's keep it simple!

Colors   I recommend that you use pans of paint rather than tubes. You can control the amount of paint you put on your brush much more easily from a pan. There are two qualities of paint: students' and artists'. I use artists'-quality watercolors, but student-grade paints can also be very good and are less expensive. I suggest that you have the following colors in your palette: Alizarin Crimson, Yellow Ochre, French Ultramarine, Cadmium Yellow Light, Cadmium Red, Hooker's Green, and occasionally Cerulean Blue (see page 18).

Brushes   The best watercolor brush you can buy is a sable brush. These are also the most expensive as they are made from real animal—but not always actually sable—hair. There are also excellent synthetic brushes on the market that cost much less than sable. I use a No.10 (the number indicates the size of the brush hairs) as my big brush, a No.6 (smaller), and a No.2 rigger for thin lines.

Paper   There are many different papers on the market. Throughout this book I have used cold-pressed watercolor paper and drawing paper. Both are high-quality, inexpensive, and available in pads of different sizes. Even experienced artists can find it awe-inspiring to

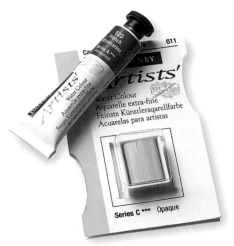

Watercolors come in tubes or pans

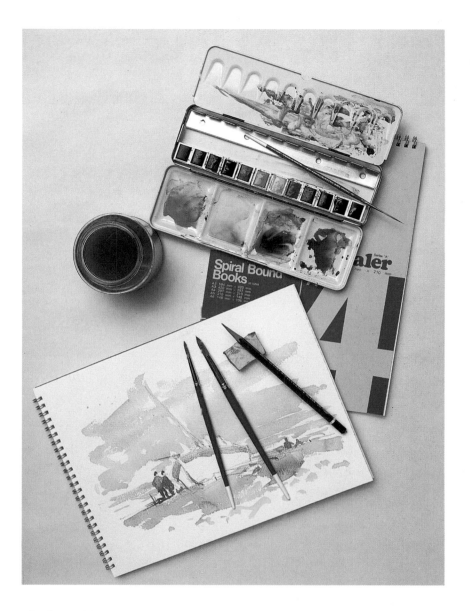

Basic equipment for a beginner

sit, brush poised, in front of a large, blank piece of paper. It would certainly frighten the hardiest of beginners! The answer is to work small to start with. Don't do any paintings larger than 10 x 15 in, but don't work in "miniature" either, as you won't get the feel for the movement of the paint and the brush on the paper. And a golden rule for watercolor painting is that you must always have your paper at an angle to allow the paint to run slowly down the page.

Other equipment A 2B pencil is a good general drawing pencil, since it is quite soft. I recommend that you use a kneaded eraser for rubbing out, as it can be used gently without causing too much damage to the paper. You will also need a water container; a jam jar is ideal for this.

Finally, before you venture outside, you should get used to working with your materials. This will make painting outdoors much more enjoyable.

TECHNIQUES

There are many ways of applying paint to paper and creating effects. I am sure that you will find some of your own as you progress. But if you practice the very important basic techniques described on the next few pages, they will show you how your brush, the paper, and the paint behave. Most importantly, you will have started on the road to watercolor painting.

Flat wash

The most fundamental technique is the wash. It is the traditional way of applying paint over a large or small area on your paper. The golden rule is to keep your paint very watery, so that it runs down and spreads on the paper. The flat wash is the first to practice.

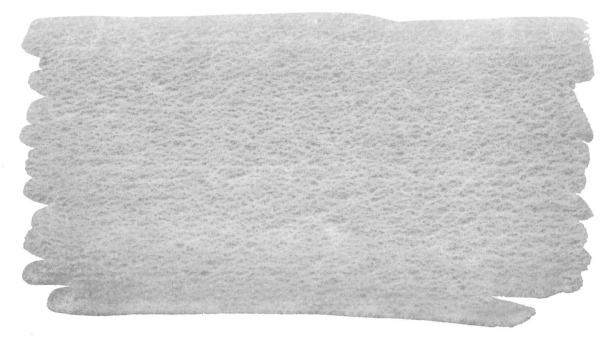

Load your large brush with watery paint. Starting at the top left-hand side of the paper, move the brush along in a definite stroke. At the end, lift the brush off the paper and start *another stroke, running it into the bottom of the first (still wet) stroke. Continue in this way, adding more watery paint to your brush as you need it.*

Graded wash

This wash is used when you want the color to get gradually paler. This technique (like all washes) can be worked small.

Graded color wash

This wash gradually changes color from top to bottom. I use this technique a great deal for painting skies.

Work exactly the same way as the flat wash, but gradually add water to the color mix in your palette to make it paler as you work down the wash.

Work the same way as the flat wash, but add different colors to the first mixed color in your palette as you work down. Keep your paint watery.

Wet-on-wet

This is a very exciting watercolor technique. Putting wet color onto wet color can lead to some of watercolor's "happy accidents." These are areas of a painting where you did not control the visual result, but it looks great. Experience will teach you how to create and control some happy accidents.

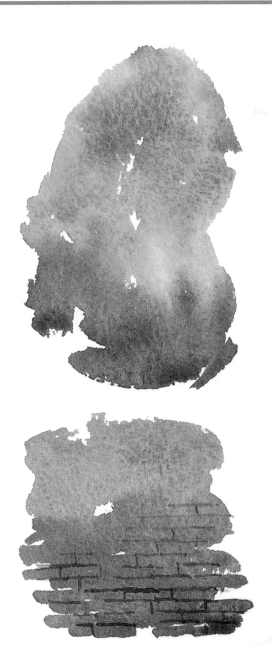

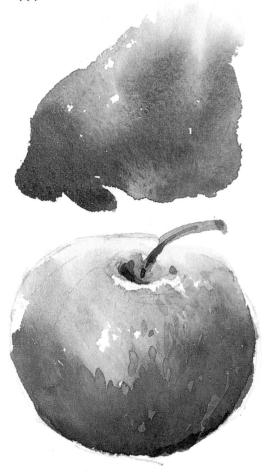

Start with yellow and then add green and finally red. The colors will all blend. When it's dry, add some stronger red to show the markings on the apple.

Let the paint run its own way, changing the color as you work. When it's dry, suggest bricks with a rigger brush. This technique is ideal for painting buildings.

Wet-on-dry

This is the way to build up a painting. Remember that if the background paint is wet, it merges, but if it is dry, you get sharp edges.

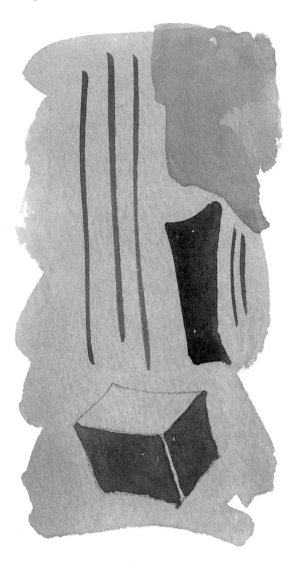

Paint a wash in any color and let it dry. Then paint on top of the dry color with different colors. Use less water on your brush when you paint thin lines, or they will spread.

Soft edges

There are times when you need to paint a soft edge instead of a sharp one. You will probably find that you use this technique quite often.

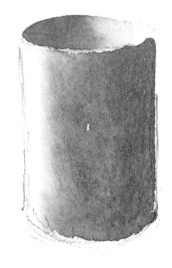

Use water for the first stroke, then continue with paint. Also try the reverse: paint a wash and finish with water. This takes lots of practice.

Dry brush

As the name implies, when you dry brush, the brush has less paint and water and is dragged along, hitting and missing the paper and leaving flecks unpainted. It also becomes a natural stroke as you run out of paint on the brush. The rougher the surface of the paper, the more exaggerated the effect will be. When you practice, try dabbing the brush on a tissue or blotting paper to remove the excess paint.

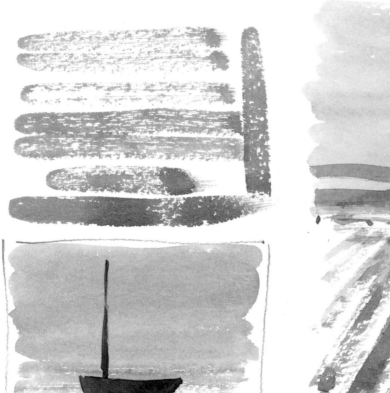

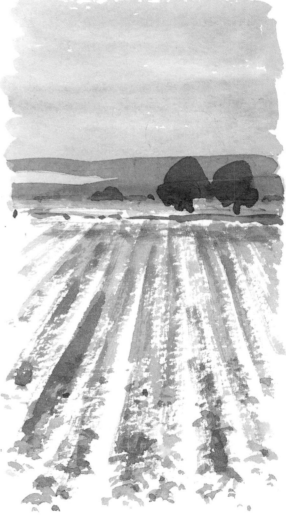

This technique is perfect for sunlit water. Just drag the brush in horizontal strokes across the paper. Keep the strokes level, or the water will appear to run downhill!

Drag the brush towards you from the edge of the field. Make the technique more pronounced in the foreground. When dry, add some blobs of darker color to this area.

Lifting out

Lifting out is removing an area of paint. This technique can be used to take off excess paint—whether it's there by accident or by design—or as part of a painting's work plan. You will never be able to lift out and leave pure white paper. The intensity of the stain left behind will depend on the color of paint and the type of paper you have used.

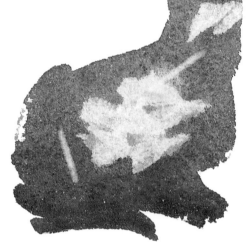

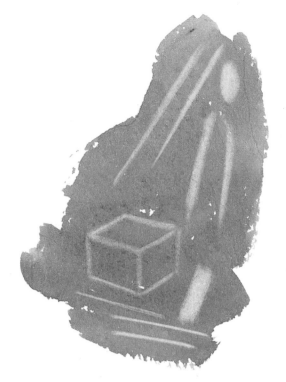

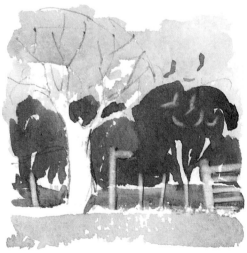

Paint an area of blue. Then, while the paint is wet, sponge out areas with a bunched-up tissue to represent clouds. This is very simple, but very effective.

With a wet brush, drag the area to be removed over and over again, then blot with tissue. Note that the tree trunk (white paper) is much whiter than the fence and gate I lifted out.

EASY COLOR MIXING

All the colors that you will need can be mixed using the three primary colors: red, yellow, and blue. Obviously, there are many different shades of red, yellow, and blue. This means that you can mix a wide range of colors.

Starter palette

When you begin painting in watercolor, I recommend that you start with the basic starter palette illustrated below, which will enable you to mix almost any color you need. These are the colors I use. In fact, for most of my painting I use only Alizarin Crimson, Yellow Ochre, and French Ultramarine to mix my colors, but I do use a green when I am painting landscapes. Throughout the book, where I discuss color mixes, I list the colors in the sequence that you should mix them.

To make colors lighter, you need to use more water in your mix (see bottom row below). In order to make the colors darker, add more paint (pigment) or less water.

Basic starter palette

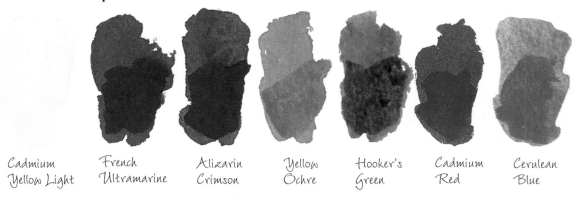

| Cadmium Yellow Light | French Ultramarine | Alizarin Crimson | Yellow Ochre | Hooker's Green | Cadmium Red | Cerulean Blue |

Basic colors with added water

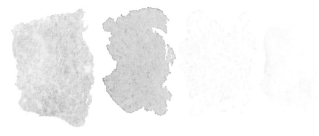

The golden rule

The most important rule to remember when mixing a color is to put the predominant color of the mix into your palette first (with water) and add smaller amounts of other colors to it. For example, if you wanted to mix a red-orange, you would put the predominant color—red—into your palette and add yellow to it. If you started off with yellow, you would have to mix a lot of red into it to overpower the yellow and make a red-orange. You would use a lot more paint, mix more than you need, lose time, and get very frustrated. So stick to the golden rule—predominant color first.

Predominant color first

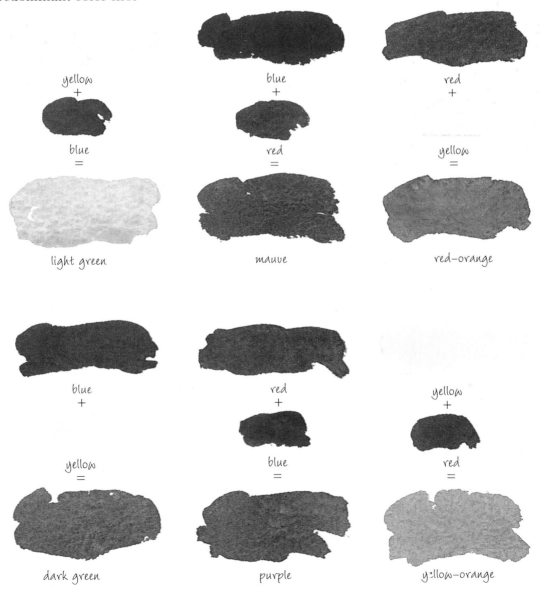

yellow
+
blue
=
light green

blue
+
red
=
mauve

red
+
yellow
=
red-orange

blue
+
yellow
=
dark green

red
+
blue
=
purple

yellow
+
red
=
yellow-orange

Mixing only three colors

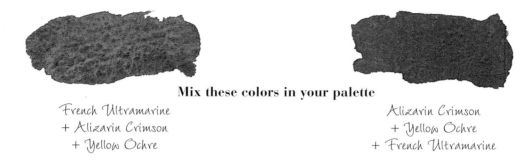

Mix these colors in your palette

French Ultramarine
+ Alizarin Crimson
+ Yellow Ochre

Alizarin Crimson
+ Yellow Ochre
+ French Ultramarine

Then add the other colors below to the above color mixes in the palette, and test the color.

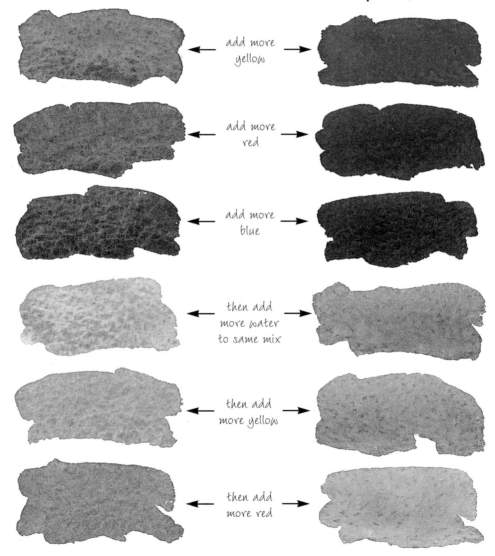

← add more
yellow →

← add more
red →

← add more
blue →

← then add
more water
to same mix →

← then add
more yellow →

← then add
more red →

More color mixing

Hooker's Green + Alizarin Crimson

Now try adding the colors below to the mix above

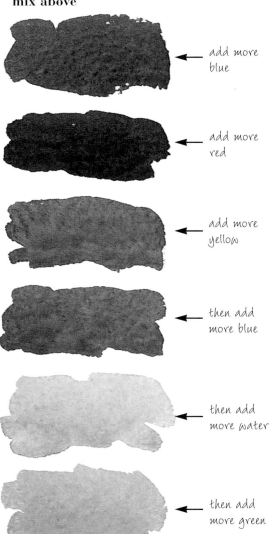

← add more blue

← add more red

← add more yellow

← then add more blue

← then add more water

← then add more green

Remember that adding water is like adding white—it makes the colors paler

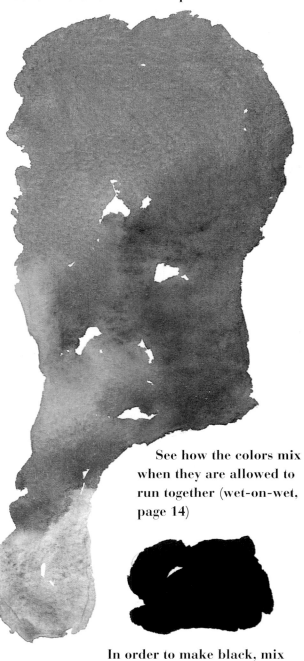

See how the colors mix when they are allowed to run together (wet-on-wet, page 14)

In order to make black, mix the three primary colors with a small amount of water

MAKING OBJECTS LOOK 3-D

This is perhaps the most important lesson to master. If your paintings don't have contrast, they will look flat, with no recognizable shapes or forms. Look at the paintings below. The objects only become realistic when you add shadows. Remember that light against dark will always show shape and form and make an object look three-dimensional.

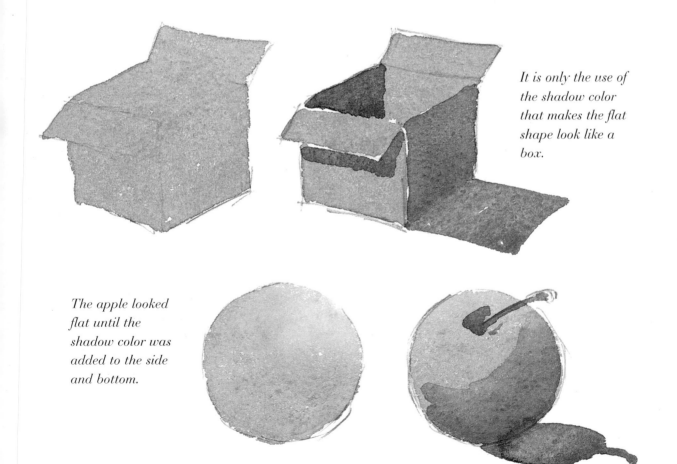

A mix of French Ultramarine, Alizarin Crimson, and a touch of Yellow Ochre will give you a good general shadow color.

It is only the use of the shadow color that makes the flat shape look like a box.

The apple looked flat until the shadow color was added to the side and bottom.

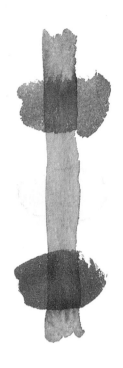

Because watercolor is transparent, the shadow color (the vertical line) allows the colors underneath to show through—but it darkens them.

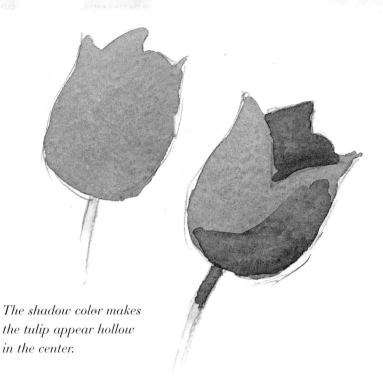

The shadow color makes the tulip appear hollow in the center.

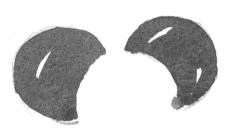

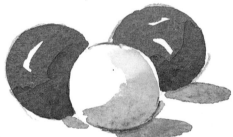

Notice how the white ball doesn't exist without the shadow. Also, the little highlight of white paper left on each ball makes them look shiny and spherical.

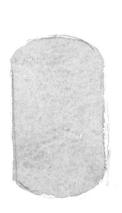

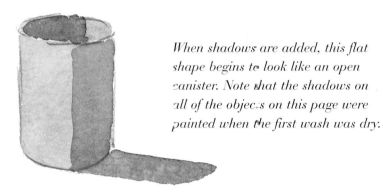

When shadows are added, this flat shape begins to look like an open canister. Note that the shadows on all of the objects on this page were painted when the first wash was dry.

FRUIT

The great thing about painting fruit is that you usually have some in the house!
You can make a picture of just one apple or a whole basket of fruit. In fact, fruit
is an ideal subject on which to practice techniques and color mixing.

Peach

Like most fruit, a peach can have many colors. These range from bright yellow to deep red-purple.
They are warm colors, and are very powerful and exciting. When you are starting out, don't try to
capture the velvety texture of the skin. Instead, concentrate on the shape and form.

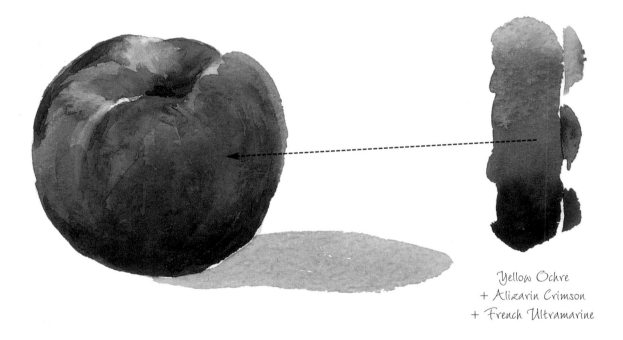

Yellow Ochre
+ Alizarin Crimson
+ French Ultramarine

*When I painted this peach, I wanted to make it
look like it was sitting on the ground. Creating
this effect took two stages. The first step was to
make the peach appear three-dimensional,*
*which I did by painting a very dark area at the
bottom of it. At that point it looked round, but
still appeared to be floating on the page.
Adding the shadow made it "sit" on the ground.*

Colorful cherries

Like peaches, cherries have vibrant colors. They are very simple to draw and there aren't any large areas to cover with paint. This is a good example of how small you can paint a wash. Although the wash used on the cherry is very small in comparison to, say, a wash on a sky, the technique is exactly the same.

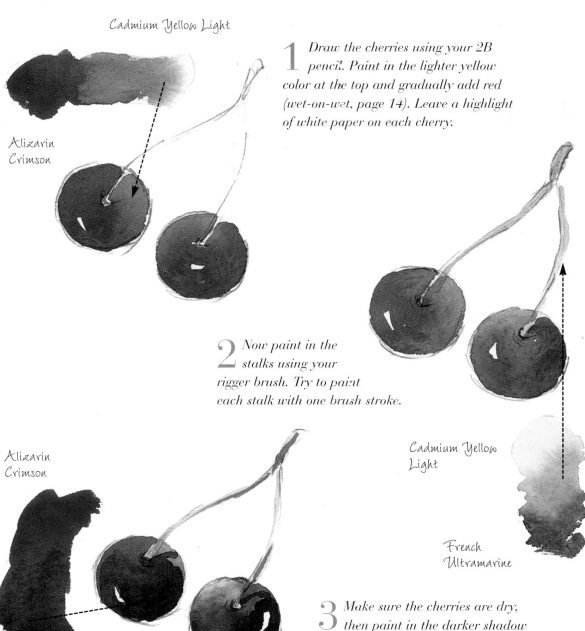

Cadmium Yellow Light

Alizarin Crimson

1 *Draw the cherries using your 2B pencil. Paint in the lighter yellow color at the top and gradually add red (wet-on-wet, page 14). Leave a highlight of white paper on each cherry.*

2 *Now paint in the stalks using your rigger brush. Try to paint each stalk with one brush stroke.*

Cadmium Yellow Light

Alizarin Crimson

French Ultramarine

3 *Make sure the cherries are dry, then paint in the darker shadow color around the bottom and right-hand side of the cherries.*

French Ultramarine

You can paint 25

Banana

This is another fruit that is not complicated to draw. When you have practiced copying mine, try painting one from life. You might find the drawing more difficult, but copying this one will have given you more confidence.

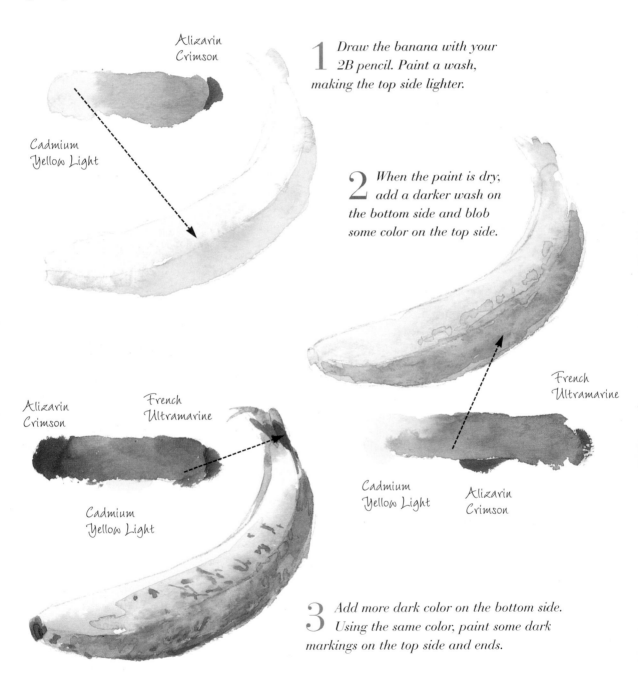

Alizarin Crimson

Cadmium Yellow Light

1 *Draw the banana with your 2B pencil. Paint a wash, making the top side lighter.*

2 *When the paint is dry, add a darker wash on the bottom side and blob some color on the top side.*

French Ultramarine

Alizarin Crimson

French Ultramarine

Cadmium Yellow Light

Cadmium Yellow Light

Alizarin Crimson

3 *Add more dark color on the bottom side. Using the same color, paint some dark markings on the top side and ends.*

Juicy grapes

These appear to be the most difficult fruit to paint, but if you look carefully, you'll find it's just like painting a lot of cherries, although the shapes and colors are different. Study them carefully before you start. Notice how in the finished stage light against dark and dark against light play an important part in making the grapes look three-dimensional (page 22).

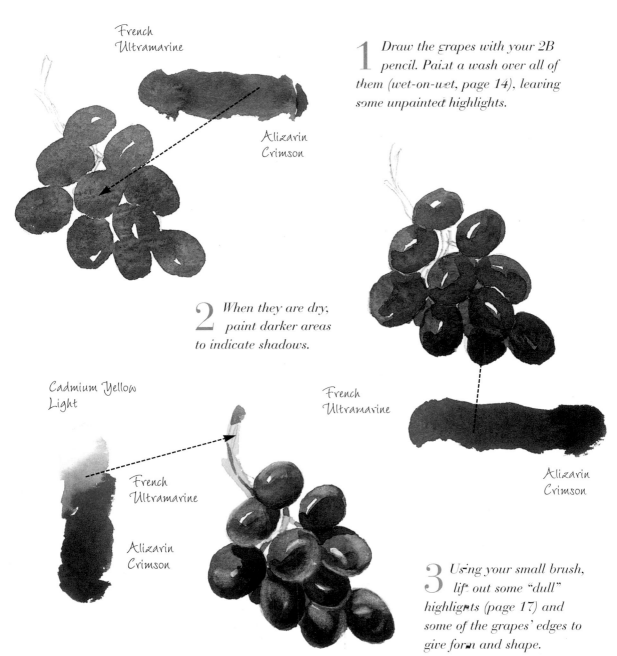

French
Ultramarine

Alizarin
Crimson

1 *Draw the grapes with your 2B pencil. Paint a wash over all of them (wet-on-wet, page 14), leaving some unpainted highlights.*

2 *When they are dry, paint darker areas to indicate shadows.*

French
Ultramarine

Alizarin
Crimson

Cadmium Yellow
Light

French
Ultramarine

Alizarin
Crimson

3 *Using your small brush, lift out some "dull" highlights (page 17) and some of the grapes' edges to give form and shape.*

DEMONSTRATION FRUIT

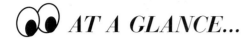 *AT A GLANCE...*

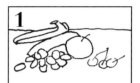 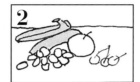 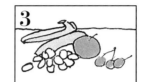 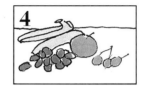

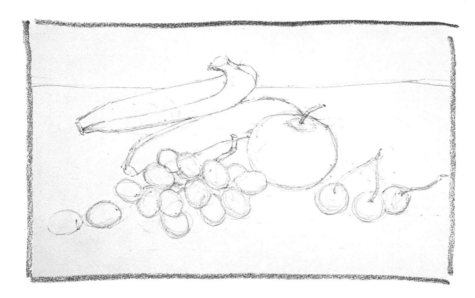

1 *Draw the fruit with your 2B pencil. Be positive with the pencil. It doesn't matter if the pencil lines still show through when the painting is finished. Start by drawing the top banana and work down to the grapes and cherries.*

2 *Using your small brush, paint the first wash on the bananas. Make the top side of the first banana lighter and the bottom side darker. This gives it form and dimension. Keep the painting simple at this stage.*

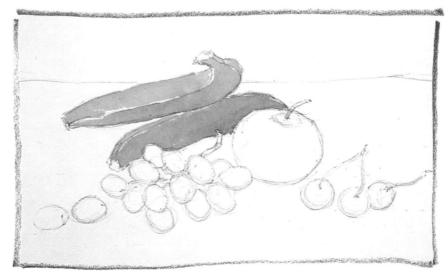

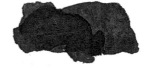

The palette

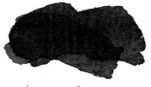

French
Ultramarine

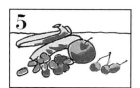

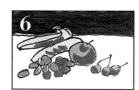

Alizarin Crimson

Cadmium Yellow Light

3 With the same brush, paint in the apple. Work your wash wet-on-wet (page 14), changing the colors as you work down the apple. Leave some unpainted highlights. Now paint the cherries in the same way, also leaving some highlights.

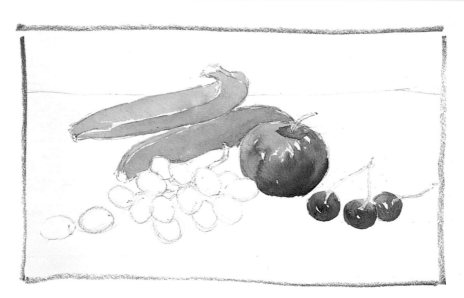

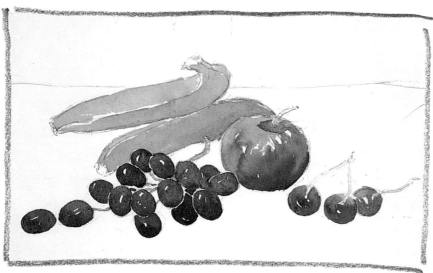

4 Continue with the first wash on the grapes. Don't worry at this stage if the fruit's colors do not look strong enough. This is only the first wash; it is the next stage that will give strength and character to the fruit.

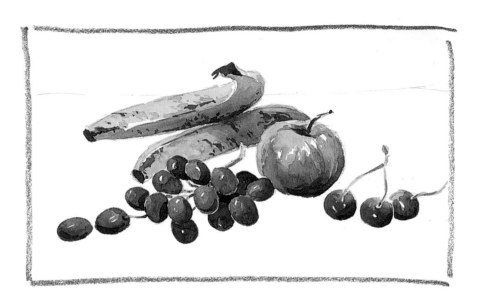

5 Paint in darker shadow areas on all the fruit, making sure they are dark enough to make the fruit appear round. Remember to follow the shape of the fruit with your brush strokes. Next, paint the dark markings on the bananas and the stalks on the other fruit.

Detail: The dark markings on the bananas are simple brush strokes, but they follow the contour of the banana. The top of the apple comes away from the banana because the apple is light against the dark shadow of the banana.

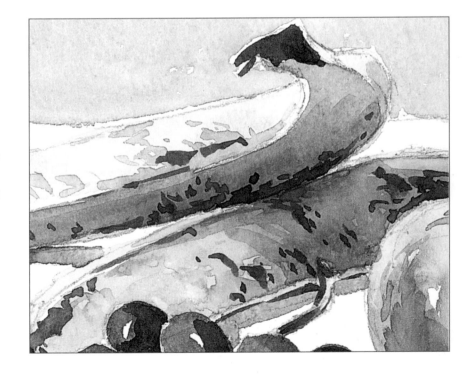

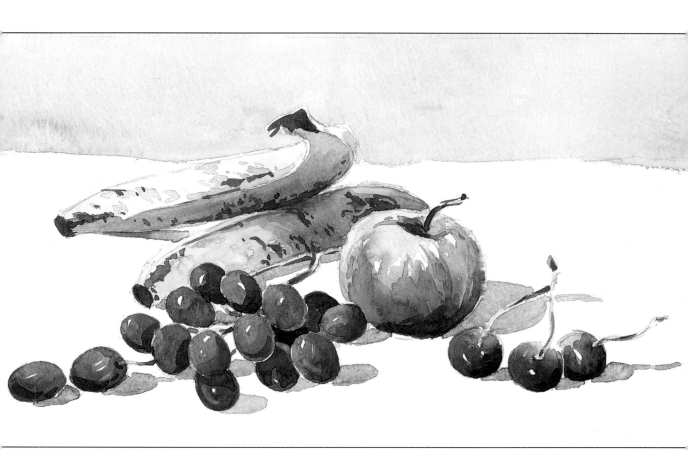

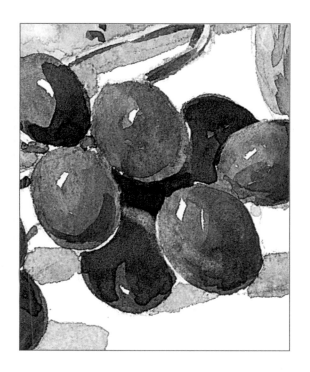

6 **Finished picture:** *watercolor paper, 7½ x 12 in. Using your big brush, paint in the background color. Now mix a shadow color with your small brush and paint in the shadows cast on the table. This makes the fruit "sit"—and not "float"—on the paper. Finally, add any dark accents you feel will help your painting.*

Detail: *Define the shapes of some of the grapes by lifting out their edges with a brush.*

VEGETABLES

Like fruit, this is a subject that you can practice painting indoors to learn the techniques and the magic of watercolor under controlled conditions. This is important at the beginning, when you want as little interruption to your concentration as possible. The painting process itself should give you enough to think about!

Green pepper

Their bright coloring, smooth texture, and bulbous shape can make peppers look like ceramic ornaments. They are a challenge to paint, so don't attempt to copy my pepper until you have tried painting the simpler vegetables on the next few pages.

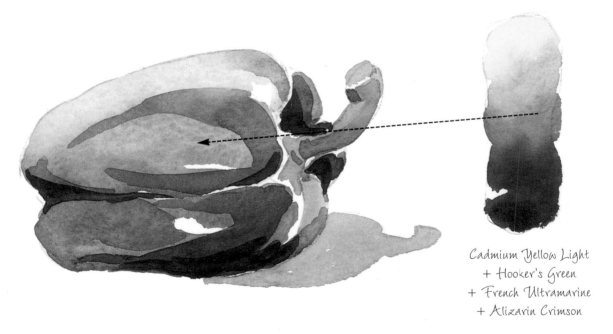

Cadmium Yellow Light
+ Hooker's Green
+ French Ultramarine
+ Alizarin Crimson

The most important part of this painting was capturing the reflected shapes and shadows. I looked at the pepper very carefully to see shapes of color and tone (light against dark).

I began by using a wet-on-wet technique (page 14). When the wash was dry, I painted darker shapes on top. Note the white paper I left for highlights.

Carrot

A carrot is easy to draw and not complicated to paint. Its main color is orange, but you still use the three primary colors to mix from. To paint the carrot, use a graded color wash technique (page 13).

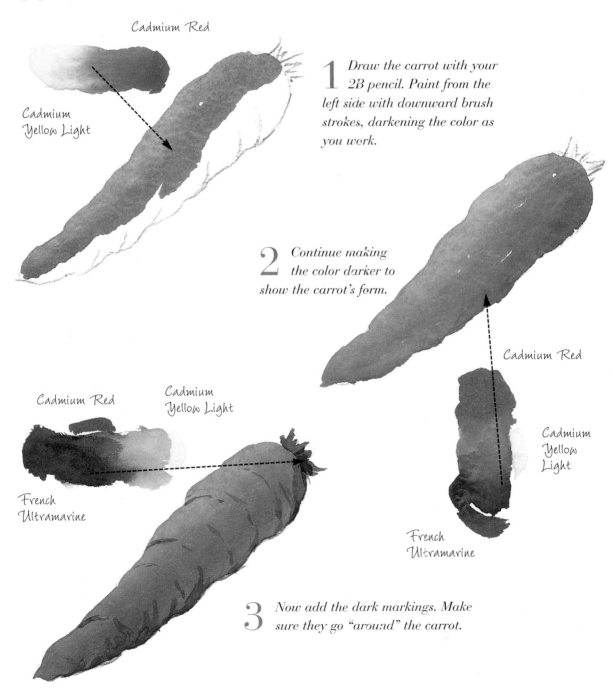

Cadmium Red

Cadmium Yellow Light

1 Draw the carrot with your 2B pencil. Paint from the left side with downward brush strokes, darkening the color as you work.

2 Continue making the color darker to show the carrot's form.

Cadmium Red

Cadmium Yellow Light

French Ultramarine

Cadmium Red

Cadmium Yellow Light

French Ultramarine

3 Now add the dark markings. Make sure they go "around" the carrot.

Radishes

Radishes are very much like cherries and grapes to paint, but they require extra drawing on the top and bottom. If you look at vegetables and fruit with an artistic eye, you'll find that many of them are very similar in shape and relatively easy to draw.

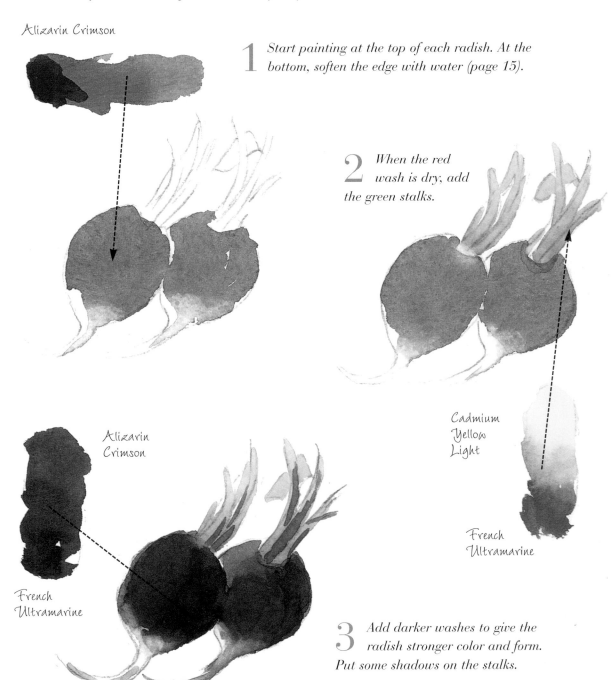

Alizarin Crimson

1 *Start painting at the top of each radish. At the bottom, soften the edge with water (page 15).*

2 *When the red wash is dry, add the green stalks.*

Cadmium Yellow Light

French Ultramarine

Alizarin Crimson

French Ultramarine

3 *Add darker washes to give the radish stronger color and form. Put some shadows on the stalks.*

Onion

By now, if you have been practicing, you will be very familiar with making objects look round in shape. The onion is another round vegetable. It lends itself very well to watercolor, because the skin can be suggested with thin, transparent washes.

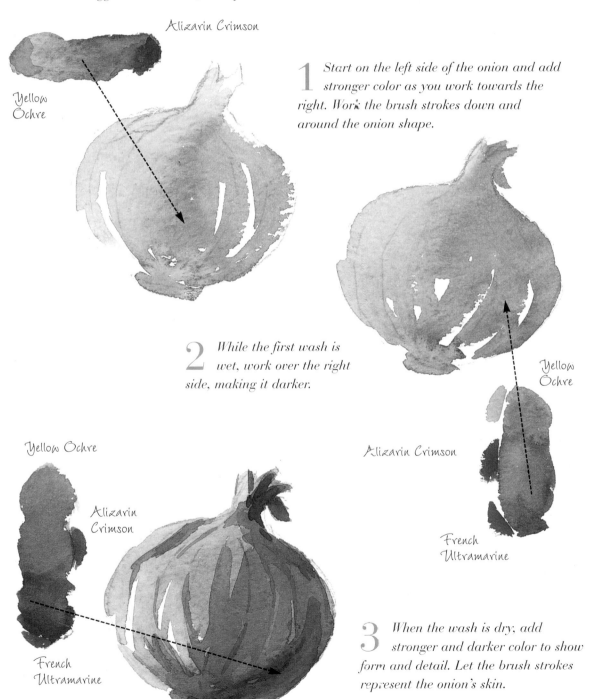

Alizarin Crimson

Yellow Ochre

1 Start on the left side of the onion and add stronger color as you work towards the right. Work the brush strokes down and around the onion shape.

2 While the first wash is wet, work over the right side, making it darker.

Yellow Ochre

Alizarin Crimson

French Ultramarine

Yellow Ochre

Alizarin Crimson

French Ultramarine

3 When the wash is dry, add stronger and darker color to show form and detail. Let the brush strokes represent the onion's skin.

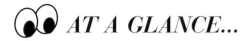

AT A GLANCE...

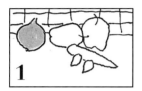
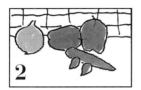
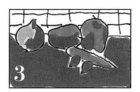
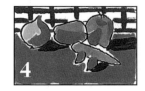

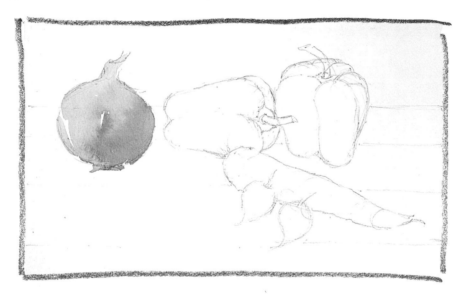

1 Draw in the vegetables with your 2B pencil. Use your big brush to mix a wash of Yellow Ochre and Alizarin Crimson. Paint the first wash on the onion, working the brush strokes down and around the entire shape.

2 Use Alizarin Crimson and Cadmium Red for the red pepper; Cadmium Yellow Light and Yellow Ochre for the yellow pepper (leave highlights); Cadmium Yellow Light and Cadmium Red for the carrot; and Alizarin Crimson and French Ultramarine for the radishes.

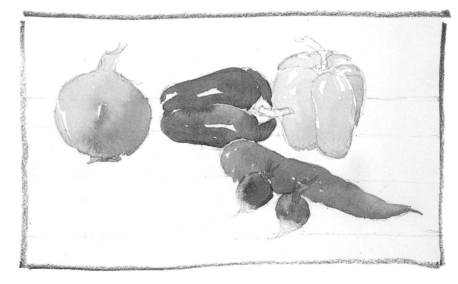

The palette

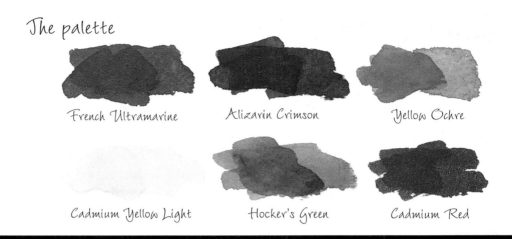

French Ultramarine

Alizarin Crimson

Yellow Ochre

Cadmium Yellow Light

Hocker's Green

Cadmium Red

3 *Now paint in the shadow (dark) areas on the vegetables, and add some modelling (darker areas to show form). When the vegetables are dry, paint in the stalks. Use your small brush for small or detailed work. Now paint in the tabletop with your big brush.*

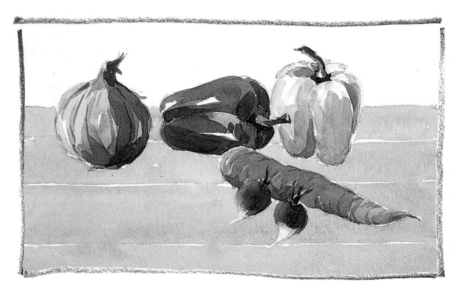

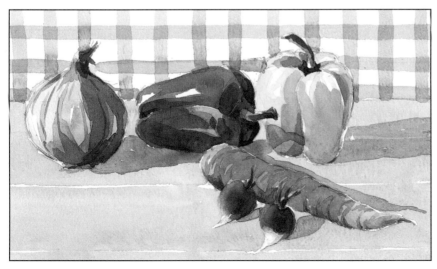

4 *Finished picture: watercolor paper, 7½ x 12 in. Using single strokes of your big brush, paint in the checked background. Then mix a shadow color and paint the shadows on the table. Notice that the red from the pepper has run into the shadow— a happy accident!*

FLOWERS

This is another subject that can be painted indoors. After copying these flowers, you can try painting one from your garden. In general, the shapes are a little more complicated than the fruits and vegetables, but if you have been practicing you shouldn't have any trouble.

Daisy

I think that the daisy is one of the most enjoyable flower shapes to paint. They are relatively simple to draw. The petals can vary in size and position, and because they are white, they can be left as unpainted paper with simple shadows painted on them.

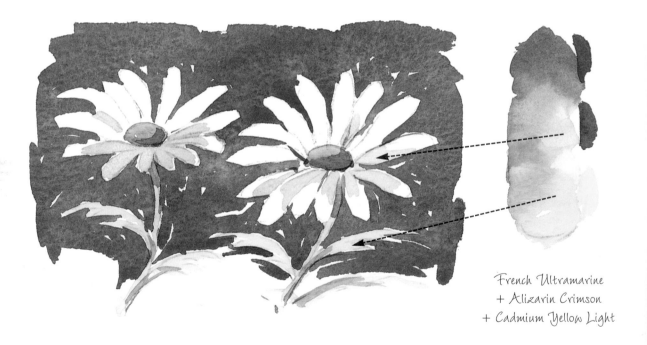

*French Ultramarine
+ Alizarin Crimson
+ Cadmium Yellow Light*

The most important part of this painting was the background of blue sky. This was done as a flat wash, but with the brush going in all directions to paint up to the petals. Remember, the secret of a good wash is to make sure your paint is very watery.

Crocus

Crocuses are small flowers, but when they come up in early spring they really make you feel as if winter has gone. They come in a variety of wonderful colors, but the yellow ones remind me most of spring.

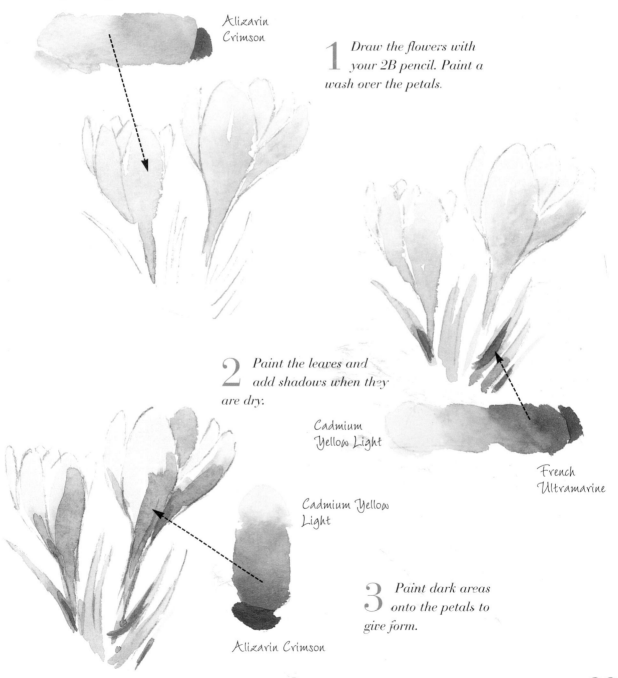

Cadmium Yellow Light

Alizarin Crimson

1 *Draw the flowers with your 2B pencil. Paint a wash over the petals.*

2 *Paint the leaves and add shadows when they are dry.*

Cadmium Yellow Light

French Ultramarine

Cadmium Yellow Light

3 *Paint dark areas onto the petals to give form.*

Alizarin Crimson

Fuchsia

If you like strong color, then the fuchsia couldn't be a better flower to paint. With its vibrant red and mauve, it is not a watercolor subject for the faint-hearted! Use bright colors and enjoy yourself!

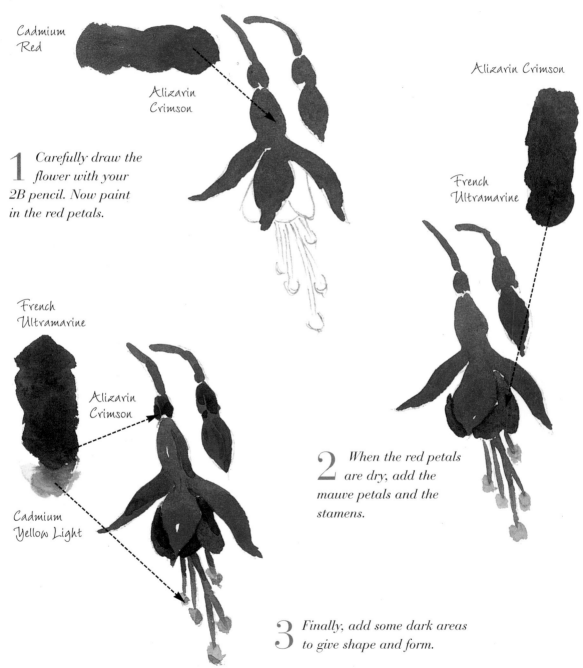

Cadmium
Red

Alizarin
Crimson

1 *Carefully draw the flower with your 2B pencil. Now paint in the red petals.*

Alizarin Crimson

French
Ultramarine

2 *When the red petals are dry, add the mauve petals and the stamens.*

French
Ultramarine

Alizarin
Crimson

Cadmium
Yellow Light

3 *Finally, add some dark areas to give shape and form.*

Snowdrop

Painting a snowdrop is like painting a crocus upside down. Because it is white like the daisy, it needs a dark background to help show its shape. With the daisy, I painted the background first, but I have painted it last with the snowdrop.

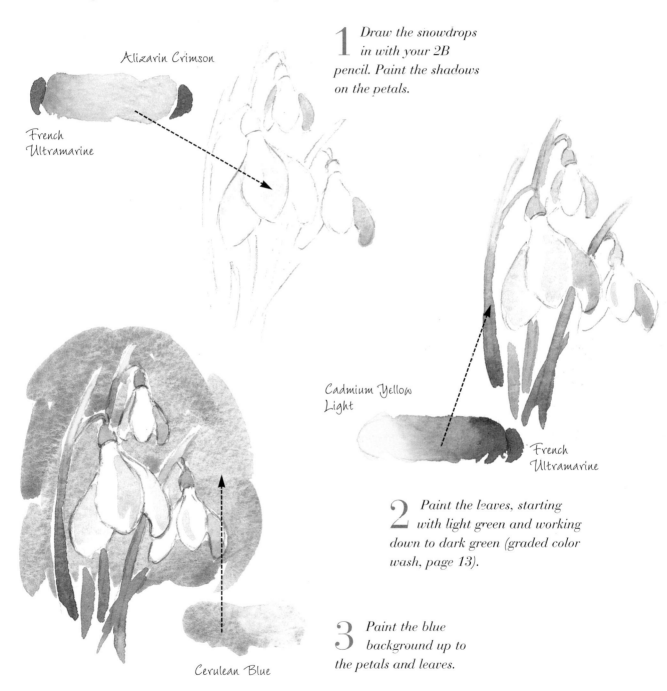

Alizarin Crimson

French Ultramarine

1 Draw the snowdrops in with your 2B pencil. Paint the shadows on the petals.

Cadmium Yellow Light

French Ultramarine

2 Paint the leaves, starting with light green and working down to dark green (graded color wash, page 13).

Cerulean Blue

3 Paint the blue background up to the petals and leaves.

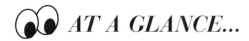

AT A GLANCE...

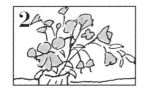 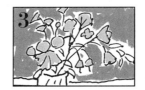 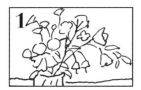 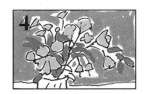

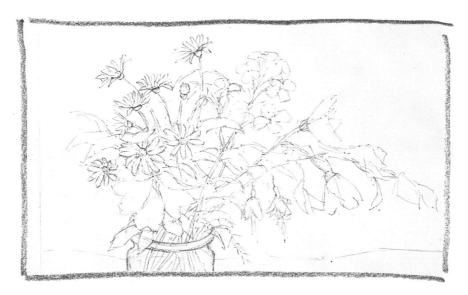

1 When the drawing looks complicated, it is important to study it before you begin. Draw in the flowers and vase with your 2B pencil. Pay special attention to the flowers; they are more important to the overall picture than the leaves.

2 Paint in the first wash on the flowers. Leave the daisies white except for the petals in shadow, then paint in the yellow centers. For the pink flowers, add just a little Cadmium Yellow Light to Alizarin Crimson.

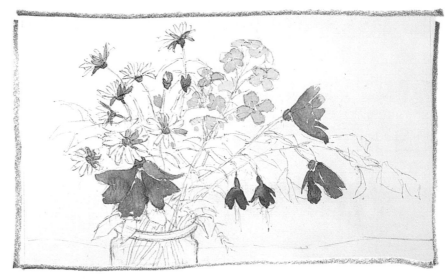

The palette

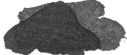

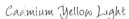

French Ultramarine   Cadmium Yellow Light   Alizarin Crimson

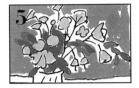

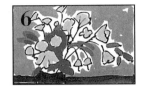

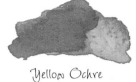

Yellow Ochre   Hooker's Green

3 *Using a mix of French Ultra-marine, Alizarin Crimson, and Yellow Ochre, paint the background with your big brush. Start at the top left and work down. Change colors as you work wet-on-wet (page 14). Use your small brush to work around the complicated areas.*

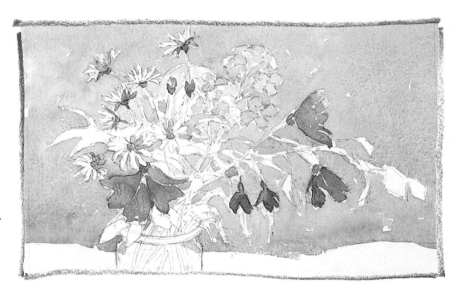

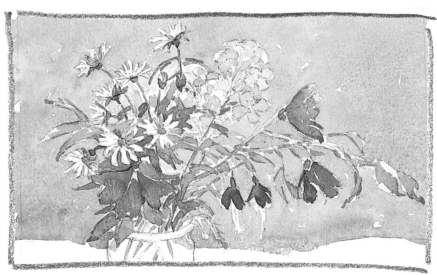

4 *When the wash is dry, paint in the leaves and stalks with a varying mix of Cadmium Yellow Light, Hooker's Green, and French Ultramarine. Work carefully around the flowers, especially the white daisies.*

You can paint 43

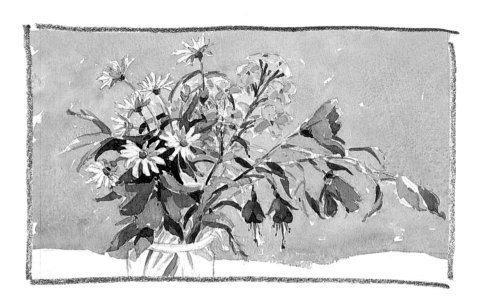

5 Using a darker green mix, paint the dark shadows and shapes of the leaves and stalks. Again, be careful when working around the flowers. Notice how the daisies now stand out more. Paint a second wash on the other flowers to give them form.

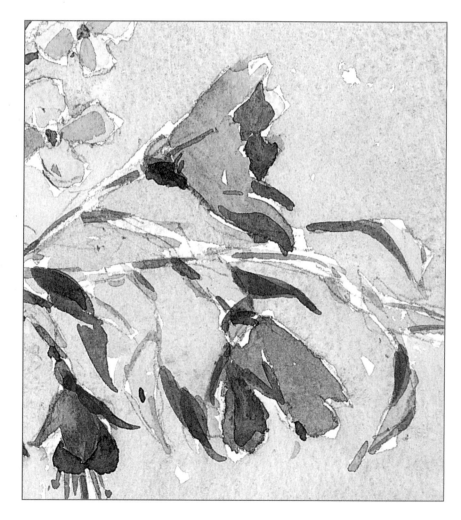

Detail: The mauve flower has been painted with only two washes. Look how the second wash —the darker one— has made the flower, which was flat in stage 2, look three-dimensional.

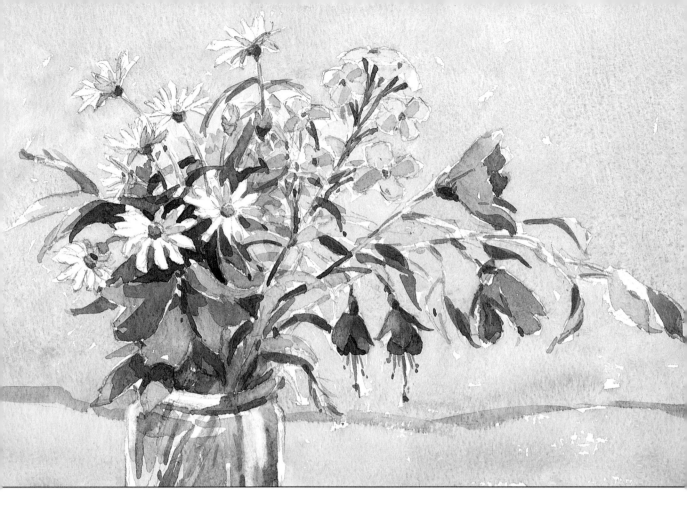

6 *Finished picture: watercolor paper, 7½ x 12 in.* Paint the orange strip in the foreground with your big brush, covering the glass vase and the edge of the background wash in places. Paint some flower stems in the vase. Finally, using the background color with a little more blue added, paint a wash on the vase, leaving highlights.

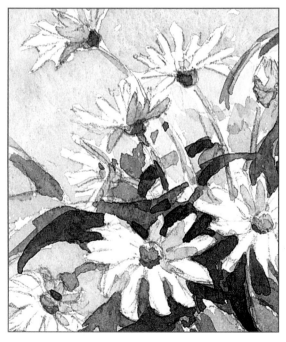

Detail: *It is important to leave white paper for the daisy petals when you paint the background. This is what gives them their shape.*

SKIES

Skies are very inspirational; they are what set a landscape painting's mood. Since you can look at them almost anytime, from outside or through a window, they are a subject that you are very familiar with. But to paint them, you need to observe them more closely.

Heavy clouds

When you practice painting skies, always suggest land, as I have done in the painting below. This gives scale to your sky. Notice how the clouds, painted very simply, get smaller and narrower the closer they are to the horizon. This gives the impression of distance. The larger, darker clouds appear to be nearer to you.

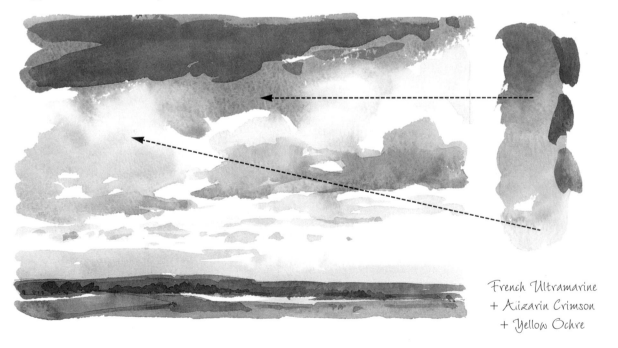

French Ultramarine
+ Alizarin Crimson
+ Yellow Ochre

I painted the blue sky first, then painted the clouds while it was wet (wet-on-wet, page 14). I allowed some clouds to run and merge with the sky. When the paint was dry, I painted darker shadows on the clouds, and the very heavy dark cloud at the top over the original blue sky.

Sunset

A sunset in any landscape painting runs the risk of looking a little over-the-top. This is simply because a real sunset is often very vivid, with vibrant colors and strong shapes. The answer, until you get more experience, is to tone down the colors.

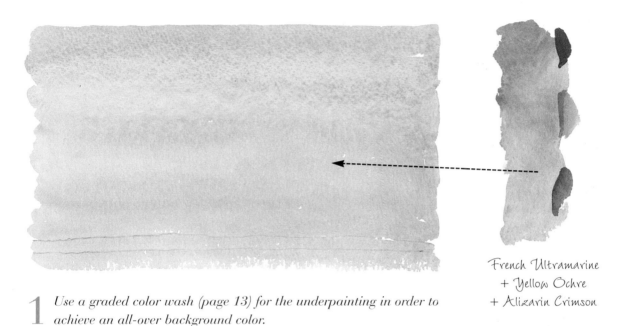

French Ultramarine
+ Yellow Ochre
+ Alizarin Crimson

1 *Use a graded color wash (page 13) for the underpainting in order to achieve an all-over background color.*

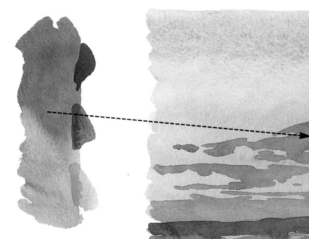

French Ultramarine
+ Alizarin Crimson
+ Yellow Ochre

2 *When the first wash is dry, paint in the clouds using positive and confident brush strokes, making them narrower the nearer they are to the horizon (wet-on-dry, page 15).*

Soft clouds

The heavy, cloudy sky (page 46) was painted with a lot of crisp edges. This sky is painted with soft edges (page 15). The clouds are further away and not overhead. There isn't a lot of definition in the clouds, which helps to make them look as if they are a long way off.

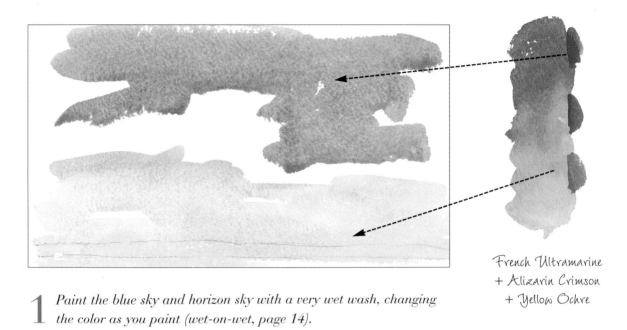

French Ultramarine + Alizarin Crimson + Yellow Ochre

1 *Paint the blue sky and horizon sky with a very wet wash, changing the color as you paint (wet-on-wet, page 14).*

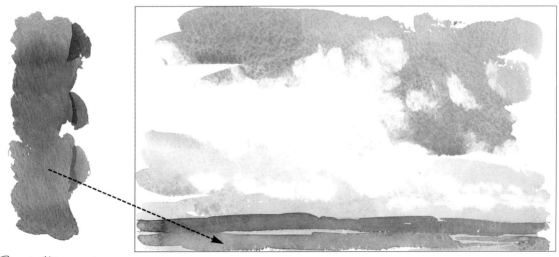

French Ultramarine + Alizarin Crimson + Yellow Ochre

2 *While the paint is still very wet, lift out the cloud shapes from the background sky with a bunched-up soft tissue (lifting out, page 17). When it dries, suggest the land.*

Rainy sky

This type of sky always looks dramatic in a painting. As you are painting wet-on-wet, there will be happy accidents, but you may also have unhappy ones. So if it doesn't work it's not your fault! Try experimenting with other colors for the sky—for example, sunset colors.

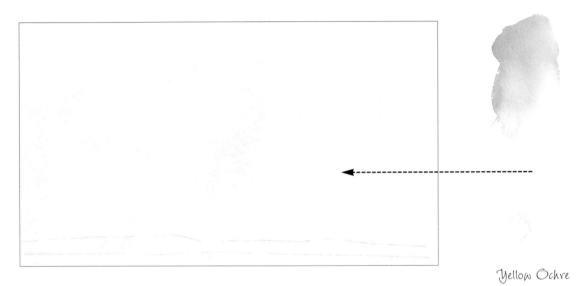

Yellow Ochre

1 *Working from left to right, paint a wash with diagonal downward brush strokes.*

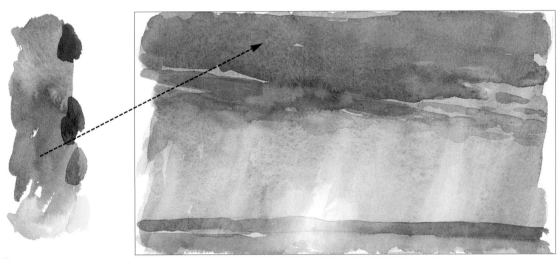

French Ultramarine
+ Alizarin Crimson
+ Yellow Ochre
+ Cadmium Yellow Light

2 *Now paint the land. When it's dry, paint a wash over everything. When the wash is dry, paint the dark clouds at the top and blend in to create the "rain" effect. Lift out sunlit areas with a brush (page 17).*

EXERCISE Paint a sky

In this exercise, the first three stages are done while the paint is wet, so you can't be interrupted while you are painting them. Have your coffee when you finish! Use my picture only as a guide—it's impossible to copy it exactly.

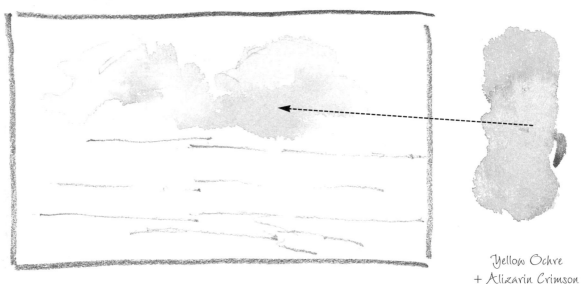

Yellow Ochre
+ Alizarin Crimson

1 *Draw the main features with your 2B pencil. Then paint the main cloud formation (wet-on-wet, page 14).*

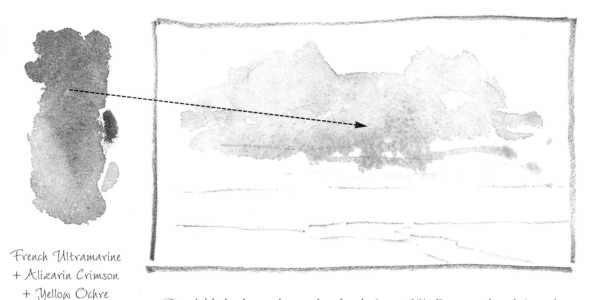

French Ultramarine
+ Alizarin Crimson
+ Yellow Ochre

2 *Add shadow color to the clouds (page 22). Put your brush into the yellow and paint down.*

50 You can paint

The palette

French Ultramarine Alizarin Crimson Yellow Ochre Hooker's Green

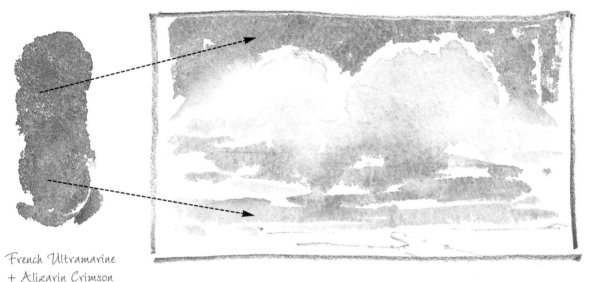

French Ultramarine
+ Alizarin Crimson

3 *Paint in the blue sky above and below the main clouds. Leave white paper edges, and let the blue merge into the clouds in some places.*

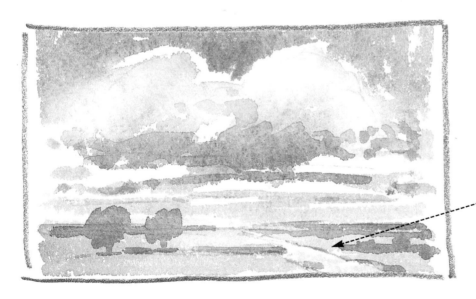

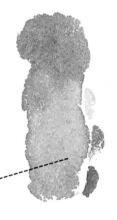

Hooker's Green
+ Yellow Ochre
+ Alizarin Crimson
+ French Ultramarine

4 *When the sky is dry, paint a stronger shadow color under the main clouds. Then paint the land.*

TREES

Trees are one of my favorite subjects. There are plenty of different shapes and sizes to work from, and of course they change their look and coloring during each of the four seasons. When you paint trees, keep them simple, and remember that like a vivid sunset, full autumn coloring can look over-the-top, so you may have to tone the colors down.

Winter willow

Willows have a very distinctive shape and can't be mistaken for any other tree. They grow in moist areas near rivers and lakes. If you're working from your imagination, don't paint willows on hills—they will look wrong!

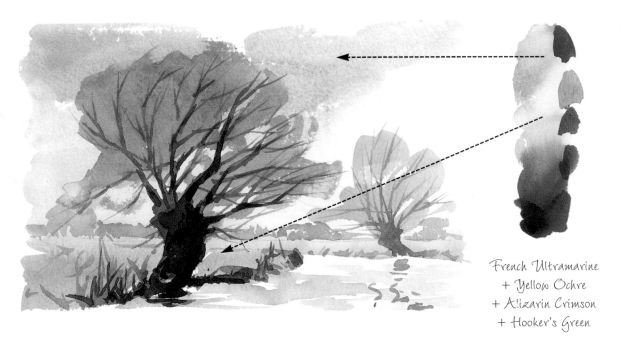

French Ultramarine
+ Yellow Ochre
+ Alizarin Crimson
+ Hooker's Green

I painted the trees on the background once it was dry. The further tree is painted in just two washes; the trunk and branches first, then a wash for the overall shape. The foreground tree was done the same way, but with more work on the trunk. Note that I have put them near water.

Winter tree

It is a good idea to start by painting a winter tree, because you can see all the branches and the way the tree forms its shape.

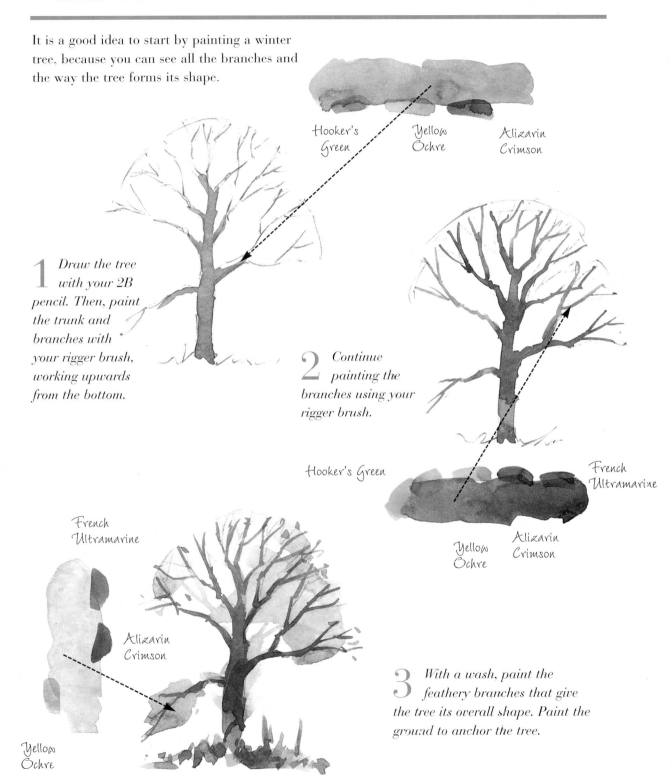

Hooker's Green

Yellow Ochre

Alizarin Crimson

1 *Draw the tree with your 2B pencil. Then, paint the trunk and branches with your rigger brush, working upwards from the bottom.*

2 *Continue painting the branches using your rigger brush.*

Hooker's Green

French Ultramarine

Yellow Ochre

Alizarin Crimson

French Ultramarine

Alizarin Crimson

Yellow Ochre

3 *With a wash, paint the feathery branches that give the tree its overall shape. Paint the ground to anchor the tree.*

Sketching trees

When you are outdoors with your pencil and sketchbook, make sketches of trees or any parts of trees that interest you. Make notes at the side or on the back of the paper. If you have your paints, then add color. These pages give you an idea of what to look for.

Trunk—make it grow
Paint plenty of growth around the base of the trunk.

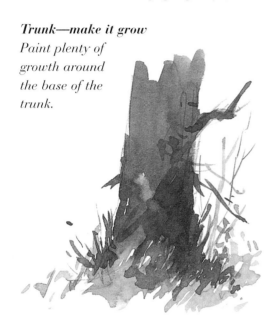

Leaves
Remember to create contrast by using dark against light. Paint light-colored leaves first, then add dark ones.

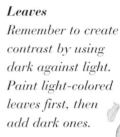
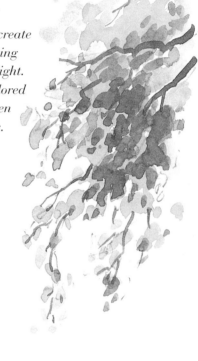

Thin branches
Use your rigger brush with plenty of water. The thinner the branch, the less water is needed.

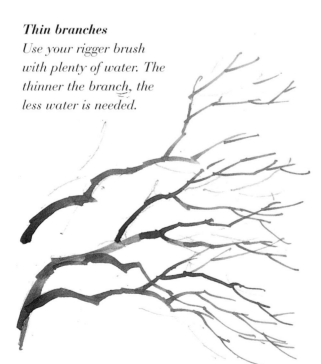

Log
Painting simple lines down the log helps to give it form and suggests bark.

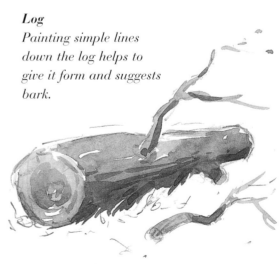

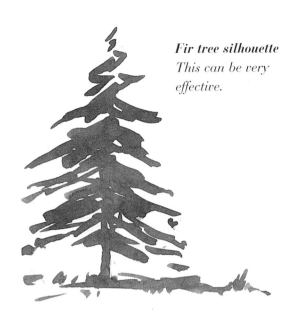

Fir tree silhouette
*This can be very
effective.*

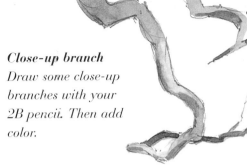

Close-up branch
*Draw some close-up
branches with your
2B pencil. Then add
color.*

Distant autumn trees
*Very simple forms can
suggest distant trees.
Paint using your small
brush with one wash.*

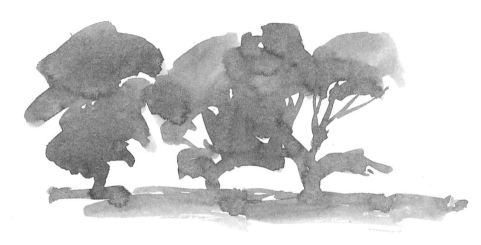

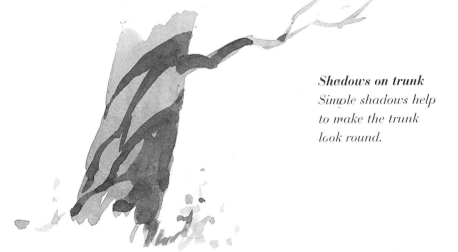

Shadows on trunk
*Simple shadows help
to make the trunk
look round.*

Paint a summer tree

Don't overwork a tree in leaf. Make sure you leave sky showing through the leaves in places, and show some branches, or the tree will look too solid. Until you have experience, don't paint trees too close-up; paint them in the middle distance like the one below.

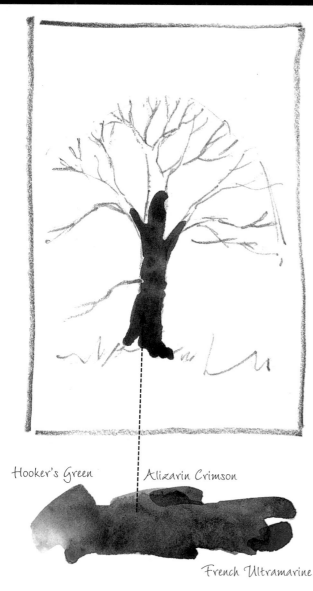

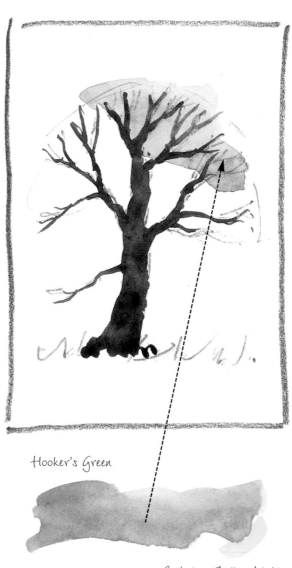

Hooker's Green

Alizarin Crimson

French Ultramarine

Hooker's Green

Cadmium Yellow Light

1 *Draw the tree with your 2B pencil. Start painting the trunk working from the bottom upwards, like you did for the winter tree (page 53).*

2 *Continue with the small branches using your rigger brush. Then start painting a wash of green from the top.*

The palette

Hooker's Green

Alizarin Crimson

French Ultramarine

Cadmium Yellow Light

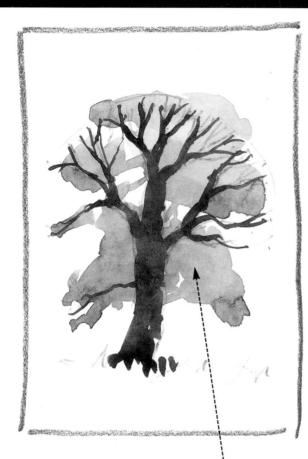

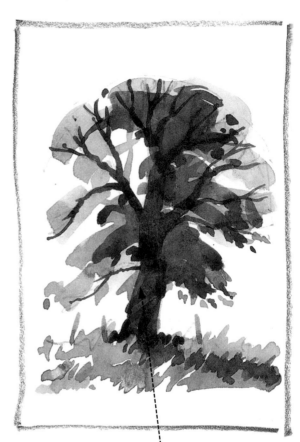

Alizarin Crimson

Hooker's Green

Hooker's Green

Alizarin Crimson

Cadmium Yellow Light

3 Continue with the green wash, using free brush strokes. Let the brush strokes dictate the shapes.

4 Using the same brush stroke, paint in the darker foliage. Go over the trunk, then paint the ground. The fence posts suggest scale.

DISTANCE AND FOREGROUND

When painting distant objects, one very important rule of thumb is that cold or cool colors—blues—recede into the distance, and warm colors—reds—advance. This means that colors you use for distant objects should be in the blue cool range and colors used in the foreground should be in the red warm range. Another important rule is that objects in the foreground are more detailed than those in the distance.

Distant village

This picture contains many optical illusions to show distance. The clouds get smaller near the horizon. The distant trees and buildings are cool blue-gray, while the foreground is painted with warmer colors. The road leads you into the distance, the distant buildings are pale and not painted in any detail, and the telegraph poles get smaller as they get further away.

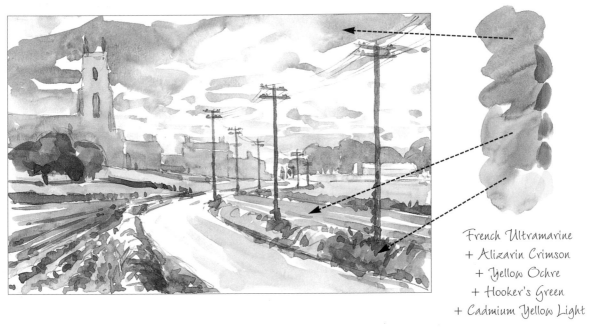

French Ultramarine
+ Alizarin Crimson
+ Yellow Ochre
+ Hooker's Green
+ Cadmium Yellow Light

The most important thing to remember is that although I could see the village in reasonable detail, I had to simplify it in my painting to keep it in the distance. Notice that there is no detail except for the church windows. The silhouette shape of the buildings is important.

Distant hills

This is a very good simplified example to show how cool colors recede. It includes another optical illusion: colors get paler as they recede into the distance. You can often see this very clearly in hilly countryside. Note the warm color used for the foreground field.

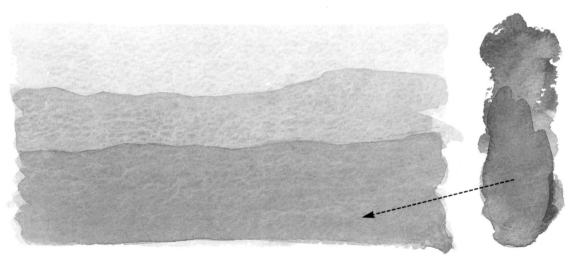

French Ultramarine
+ Alizarin Crimson
+ Yellow Ochre

1 *Paint a pale blue wash down to the field. When it's dry, paint over the lower two-thirds of it with a darker wash. Finally, when this is dry, paint a third, even darker wash over the bottom section of the painting.*

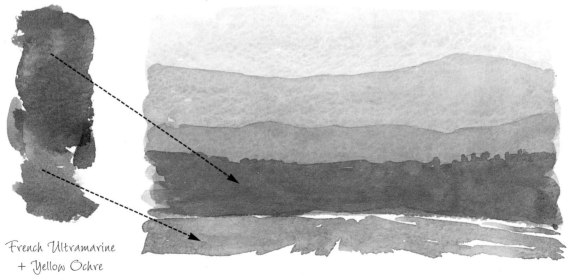

French Ultramarine
+ Yellow Ochre
+ Alizarin Crimson

2 *Paint in the last dark hill. Let the brush bounce around at the top to represent simple silhouettes of trees. Finally, paint the warm foreground field.*

Foreground path with fence

One of the biggest problems that beginners have with the foreground is that they try to include too much detail. Keep the foreground simple. Look how simple mine is in the exercises on these pages, and on page 58.

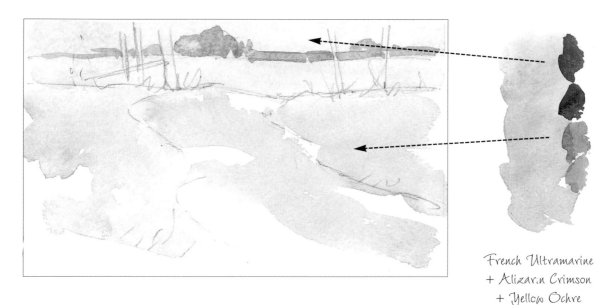

French Ultramarine
+ Alizarin Crimson
+ Yellow Ochre
+ Hooker's Green

1 *Paint a wash from top to bottom, using plenty of water and changing the color as you go. When dry, paint in the distant trees.*

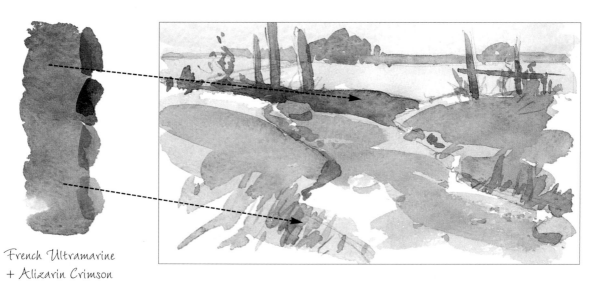

French Ultramarine
+ Alizarin Crimson
+ Yellow Ochre
+ Hooker's Green

2 *Paint stronger greens and browns to show simple form. When dry, paint in the fence and shadows.*

Foreground snow

Watercolor is a great medium for painting snow. Let the white paper be your lightest snow areas and add washes to show form and shape. Keep the snow simple.

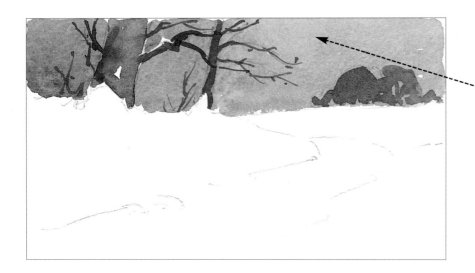

French Ultramarine
+ Alizarin Crimson
+ Yellow Ochre
+ Hooker's Green

1 Paint in the sky, leaving white paper where you will put the big tree trunk. When dry, paint in the trees. Leave an area of unpainted paper at the bottom of each trunk to represent snow.

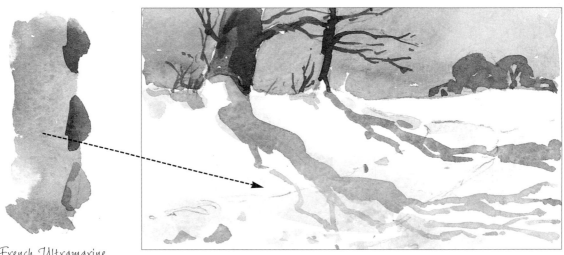

French Ultramarine
+ Alizarin Crimson
+ Yellow Ochre

2 With free, simple brush strokes, paint washes to show the contours of the snow. When dry, paint in the tree shadows. Remember to keep it simple.

DEMONSTRATION **LANDSCAPE**

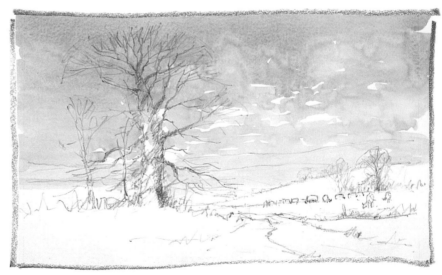 *AT A GLANCE...*

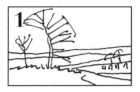
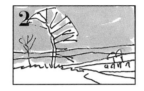
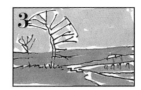
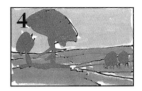

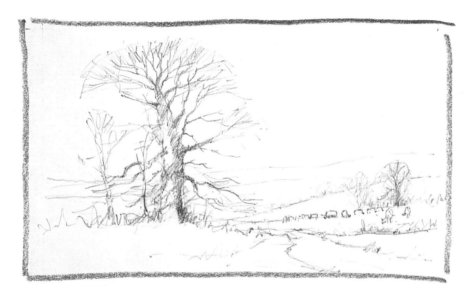

1 *Draw this landscape on drawing paper with your 2B pencil. Shade in the shadow areas on the trees. This shading and pencil work will help to make the painting look more "alive" and complicated when you paint it. I work like this a lot when I am painting outdoors.*

2 *Using your big brush, paint a wash for the sky, changing the color as you get nearer to the horizon. Leave some flecks of white paper showing to represent distant clouds. Cover the distant hills with this wash. Use French Ultramarine, Alizarin Crimson, and Yellow Ochre for this wash.*

The palette

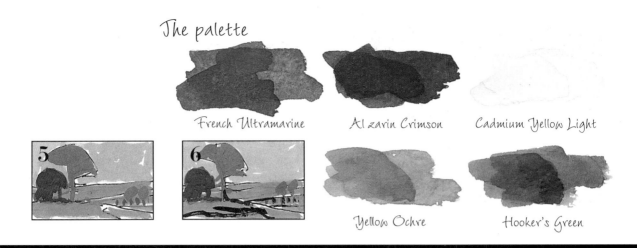

French Ultramarine

Alizarin Crimson

Cadmium Yellow Light

Yellow Ochre

Hooker's Green

3 Using your big brush, paint the distant hills in two washes, as you did on page 59. Don't paint over the tree trunk. Now paint the distant fields, working down to the foreground field. Leave the cows unpainted. Note how freely this was painted.

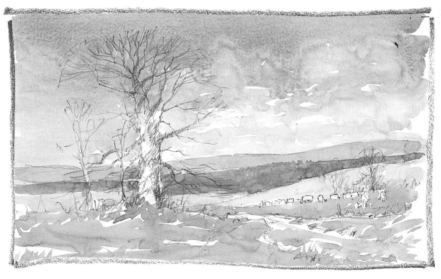

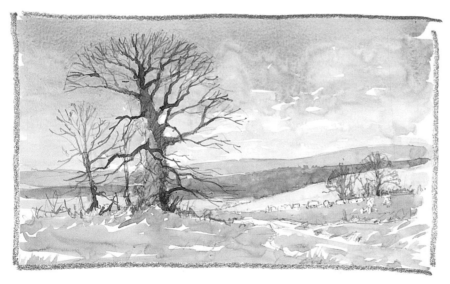

4 Paint in the main trees. Use your small brush for the main trunk and large branches, and your rigger brush for the small branches and small trees. Notice how I have painted the left-hand side of the main tree trunk paler to show the sunlight on it.

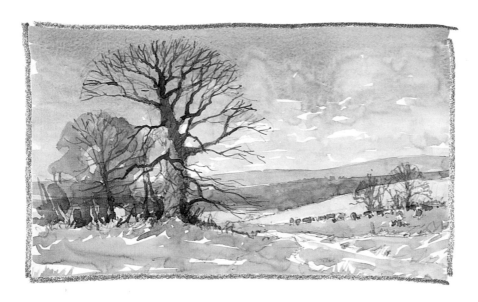

5 Now, with a wash of Cadmium Yellow Light, Alizarin Crimson, and French Ultramarine, paint the autumn color on the trees at the left. Let the colors mix on the paper (wet-on-wet, page 14). Notice how the cool colors (hills) recede and the warm colors (trees and foreground) come forward.

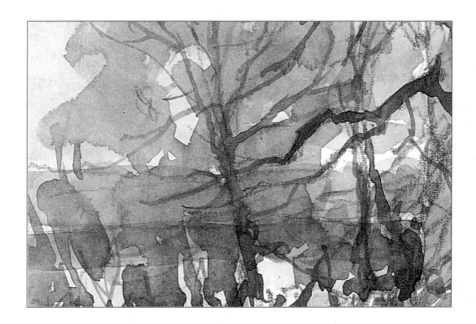

Detail: Paint the autumn colors in one wash over all the branches. Look how I have allowed areas of the background (sky and hills) to show through. Don't try to copy my painting: it's impossible. Let this happen accidentally as you paint.

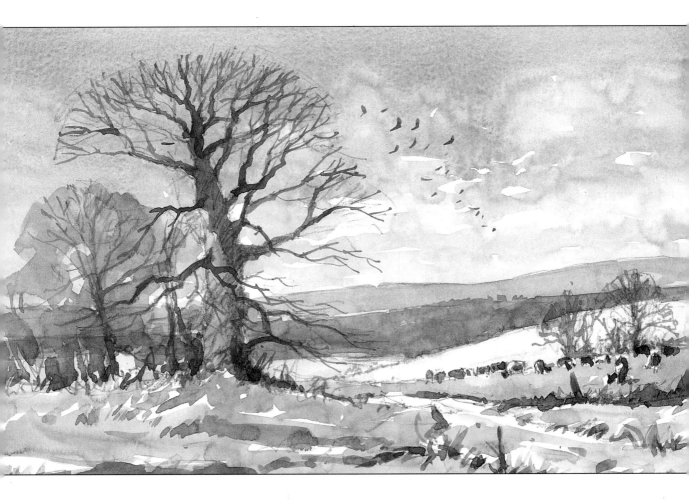

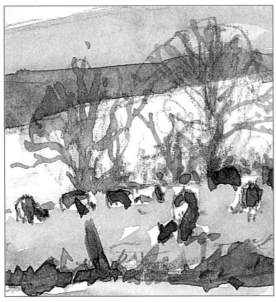

6 **Finished picture:** *drawing paper,
7½ x 12 in. Suggest a simple foreground
with shadows. Paint the cows darker and add
the birds. This painting looks difficult, but it is
built up using simple techniques. It is only
when everything is put together that it looks
complicated.*

Detail: *Notice how
freely the cows and
trees have been
painted. Also, look
how the distant hills
recede.*

ANIMALS AND BIRDS

If you enjoy painting landscapes, then you will need to practice painting the landscape's animals and birds. Some require more drawing than others. If you find that these are too difficult to begin with, don't put them in your picture until you feel more confident. The secret of painting animals is to practice painting them from life or from photographs until you are familiar with them.

Cows

Cows are perhaps the most common animals seen in the countryside. Putting any kind of animal into a landscape painting, but especially cows, gives the picture atmosphere and life.

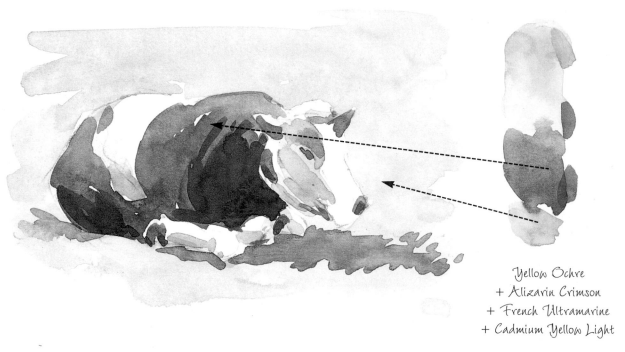

Yellow Ochre
+ Alizarin Crimson
+ French Ultramarine
+ Cadmium Yellow Light

The drawing was important, but even more critical was the way I created contrast to show form and make the cow look solid. I made the black areas on top "light," then painted darker black areas elsewhere. I left the whitest whites as paper. The shadow keeps the cow from floating.

Sheep

Sheep are perhaps the easiest animals to paint within a landscape. In the distance, they can be suggested by just leaving small areas of unpainted paper. Even when they are closer, the drawing is easy and they are simple to paint.

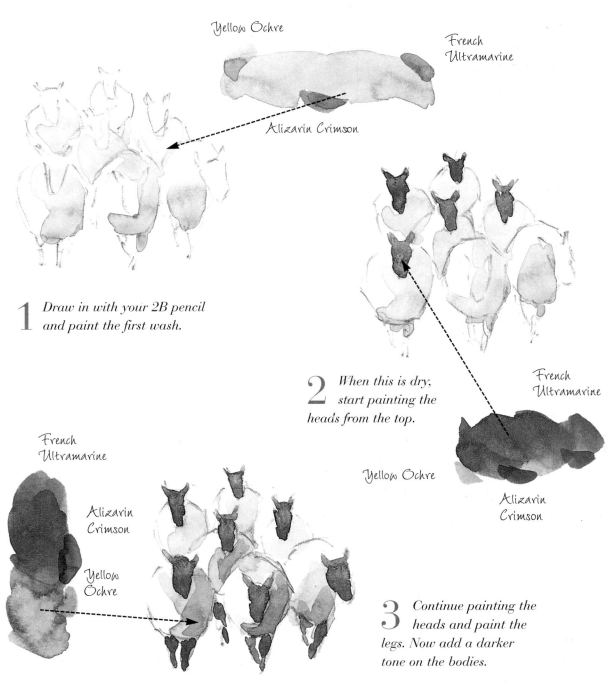

Yellow Ochre

French Ultramarine

Alizarin Crimson

1 *Draw in with your 2B pencil and paint the first wash.*

2 *When this is dry, start painting the heads from the top.*

French Ultramarine

Yellow Ochre

Alizarin Crimson

French Ultramarine

Alizarin Crimson

Yellow Ochre

3 *Continue painting the heads and paint the legs. Now add a darker tone on the bodies.*

Sheepdog

Sheepdogs are usually seen around farms and are typical farm working dogs. A sheepdog has a unique visual character with its large, shaggy white tail and chest.

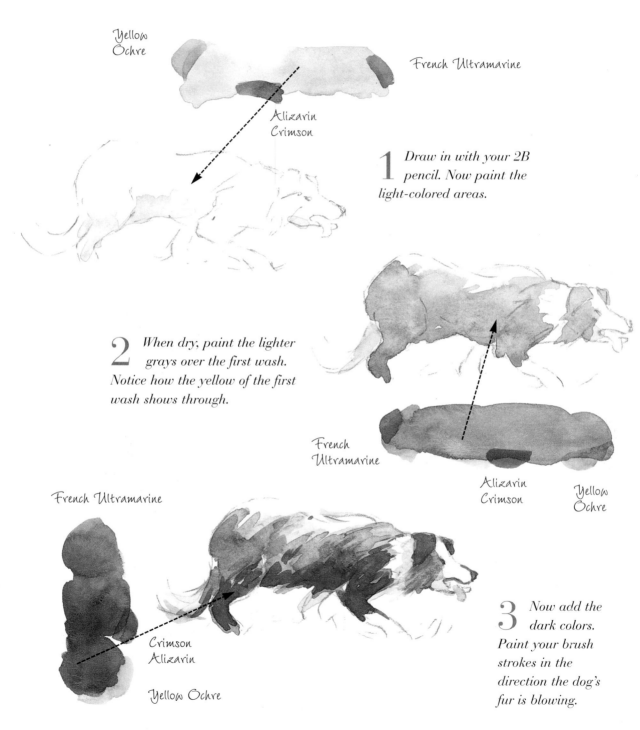

Yellow Ochre

French Ultramarine

Alizarin Crimson

1 Draw in with your 2B pencil. Now paint the light-colored areas.

2 When dry, paint the lighter grays over the first wash. Notice how the yellow of the first wash shows through.

French Ultramarine

Alizarin Crimson

Yellow Ochre

French Ultramarine

Crimson Alizarin

Yellow Ochre

3 Now add the dark colors. Paint your brush strokes in the direction the dog's fur is blowing.

Farm horse

The horse is far more complicated than the sheep or dog, but it is worth practicing as it adds a certain nostalgia to a landscape painting. Practice from life or photographs, but first copy this one, which is wearing a harness—it's a challenge!

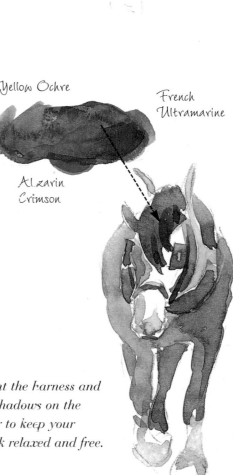

1 *Draw the horse carefully with your 2B pencil. Then paint the first wash.*

Yellow Ochre

Alizarin Crimson

French Ultramarine

2 *Paint the brass on the harness and the shadows on the horse's hooves.*

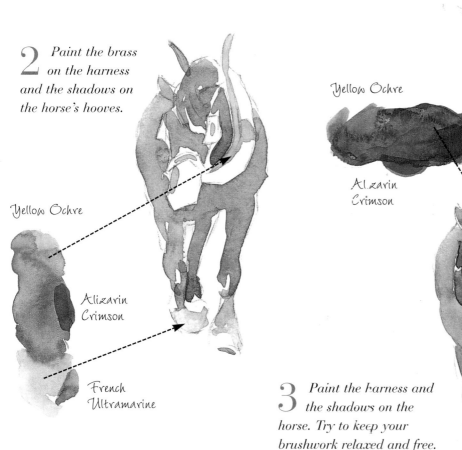

Yellow Ochre

Alizarin Crimson

French Ultramarine

Yellow Ochre

French Ultramarine

Alizarin Crimson

3 *Paint the harness and the shadows on the horse. Try to keep your brushwork relaxed and free.*

Duck

Where you have water in your landscape, a duck is always useful for adding life to the scene. I find that they have more character out of water than swimming in it. In fact, they can make quite a fun element in a painting.

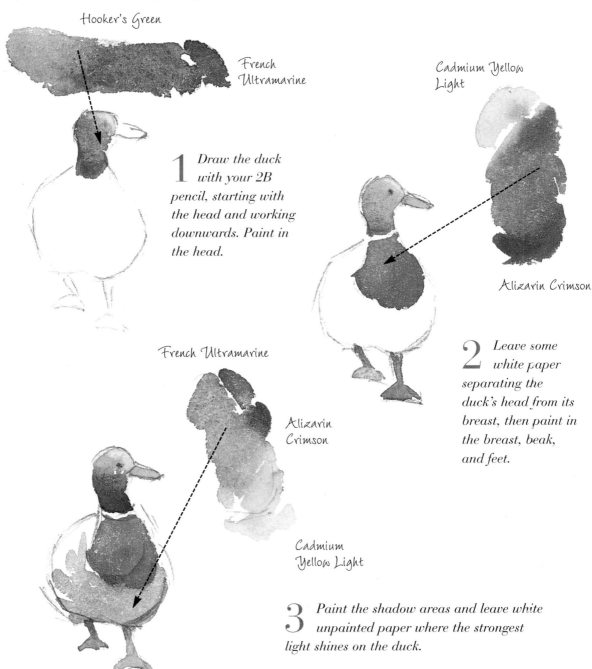

Hooker's Green

French Ultramarine

Cadmium Yellow Light

Alizarin Crimson

1 Draw the duck with your 2B pencil, starting with the head and working downwards. Paint in the head.

2 Leave some white paper separating the duck's head from its breast, then paint in the breast, beak, and feet.

French Ultramarine

Alizarin Crimson

Cadmium Yellow Light

3 Paint the shadow areas and leave white unpainted paper where the strongest light shines on the duck.

Sketching birds

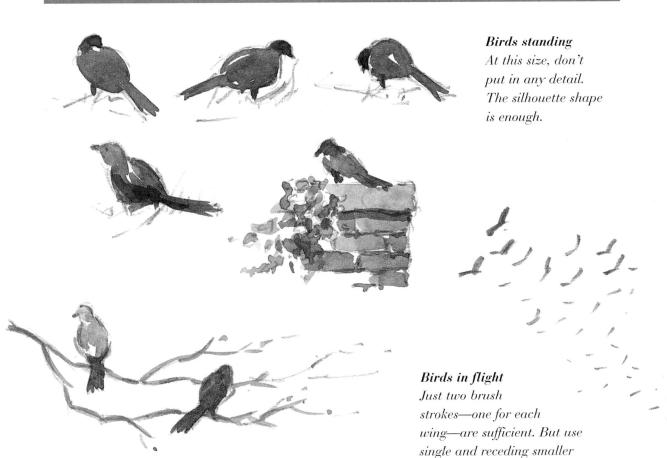

Birds standing
At this size, don't put in any detail. The silhouette shape is enough.

Birds in flight
Just two brush strokes—one for each wing—are sufficient. But use single and receding smaller strokes for the birds in the distance.

Birds on branches
Again, the silhouette shape is enough.

Pheasants
The long tail and bright colors make these birds very enjoyable to paint.

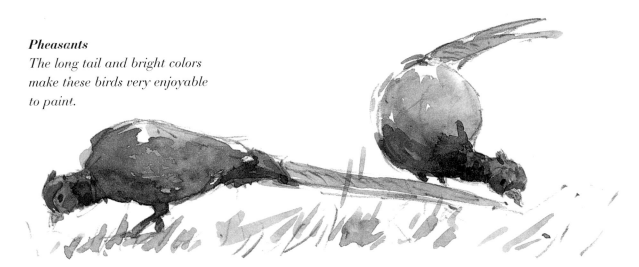

EXERCISE Paint animals

If you look at each cow individually, this painting is not as daunting as it seems. Paint each cow separately, and the background and foreground will hold the painting together. Notice how the foreground is painted very simply (page 60).

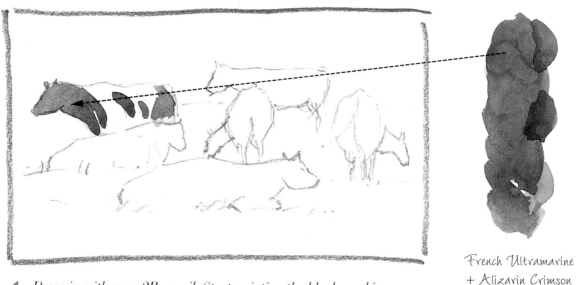

French Ultramarine
+ Alizarin Crimson
+ Yellow Ochre

1 *Draw in with your 2B pencil. Start painting the black markings on the top left-hand cow.*

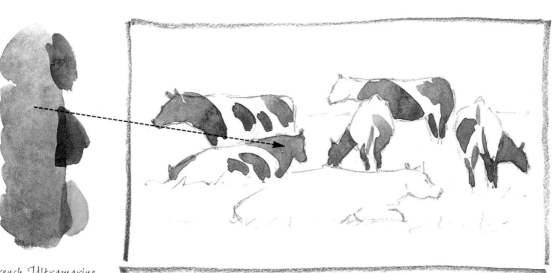

French Ultramarine
+ Alizarin Crimson
+ Yellow Ochre

2 *Continue painting the black markings. Make sure you curve them around the cows' bodies, or your cows will look flat!*

The palette

  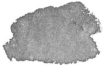 

French Ultramarine Alizarin Crimson Yellow Ochre Hooker's Green Cadmium Yellow Light

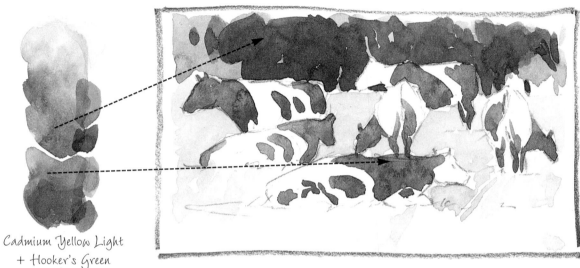

Cadmium Yellow Light
+ Hooker's Green
+ French Ultramarine
Yellow Ochre
+ Alizarin Crimson

3 *Paint the brown-and-white cow. Note how I put this "warm-colored" cow in the foreground (page 58). Paint in the grass and background.*

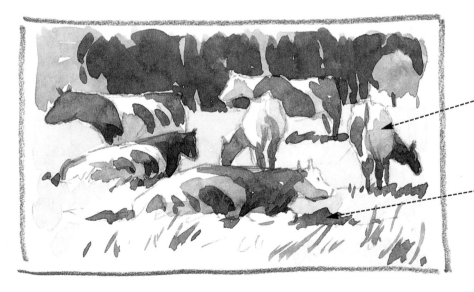

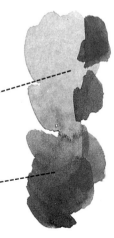

French Ultramarine
+ Alizarin Crimson
+ Yellow Ochre

4 *Paint darker shadows on the cows and grass. Notice that I have left the brown cow's eye in pencil because it looks fine this way. Keep it simple!*

PEOPLE

Painting people—or "life painting," as it is known—is very exciting and complex. Here I want to show you how you can simplify people so that you can put them in your paintings. This is not a lesson in figure drawing; it is a lesson in simplification.

Animation

If possible, you want to animate your people. One simple way of doing this is with the head. On the right are five bald heads. Below them I have added hair using just one brush stroke. Now they are looking in a definite direction.

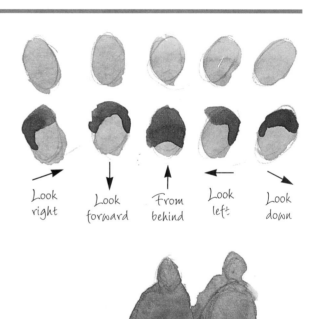

Look right   Look forward   From behind   Look left   Look down

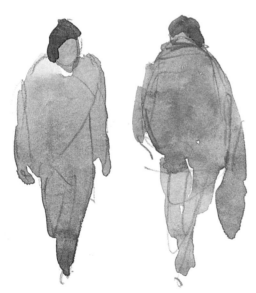

The two people above are looking at each other as they pass. I depicted this by tilting their heads and adding the hair with a single brush stroke. I started the body at the top and worked down in one movement, adding a change of color as I went (wet-on-wet, page 14).

These silhouette figures were painted from the head downwards in one movement. Let them merge together where they touch, and don't put feet on them.

Mother and child

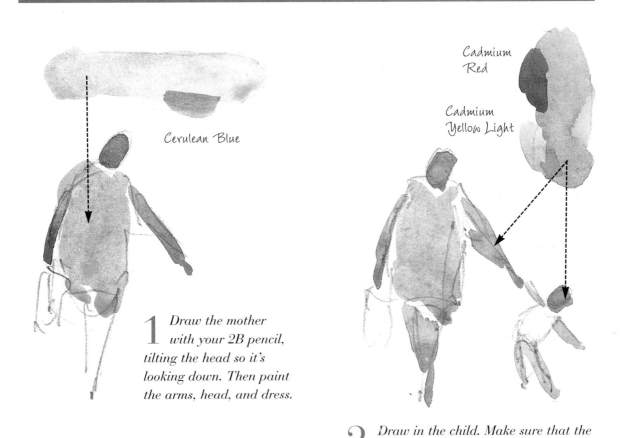

Cerulean Blue

1 Draw the mother with your 2B pencil, tilting the head so it's looking down. Then paint the arms, head, and dress.

Cadmium Red

Cadmium Yellow Light

2 Draw in the child. Make sure that the head is looking up at the mother. Then paint the arms and legs. Remember, no feet!

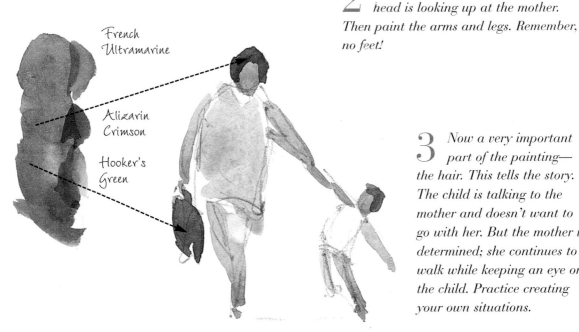

French Ultramarine

Alizarin Crimson

Hooker's Green

3 Now a very important part of the painting— the hair. This tells the story. The child is talking to the mother and doesn't want to go with her. But the mother is determined; she continues to walk while keeping an eye on the child. Practice creating your own situations.

EXERCISE Paint people

A group of people can give life and interest to a painting. But keep them simple. Don't put in detail or they will jump out of the picture. Don't forget to animate their heads.

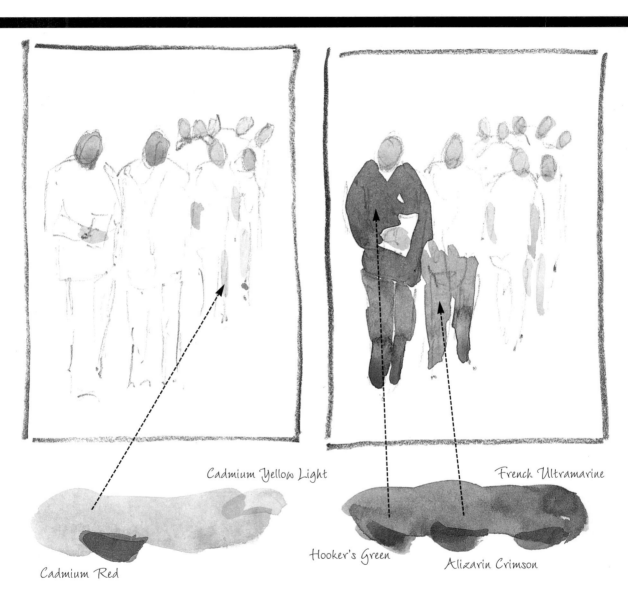

Cadmium Yellow Light

Cadmium Red

Hooker's Green

French Ultramarine

Alizarin Crimson

1 *Draw the figures using a 2B pencil, but don't draw any detail. Paint in their heads, arms, and legs.*

2 *Now paint in the two foreground figures. Notice how the green jacket has run into the blue pants. This helps to keep them "free."*

The palette

 Cadmium Red

 Cadmium Yellow Light

 Hooker's Green

 Alizarin Crimson

 French Ultramarine

 Yellow Ochre

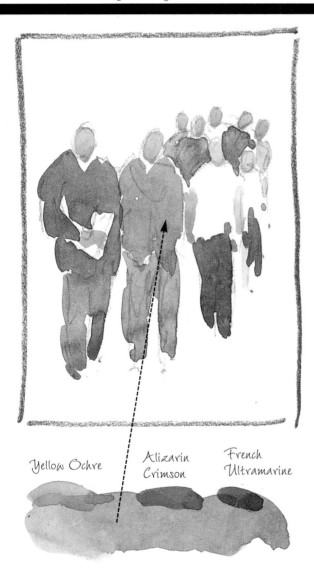

Yellow Ochre   Alizarin Crimson   French Ultramarine

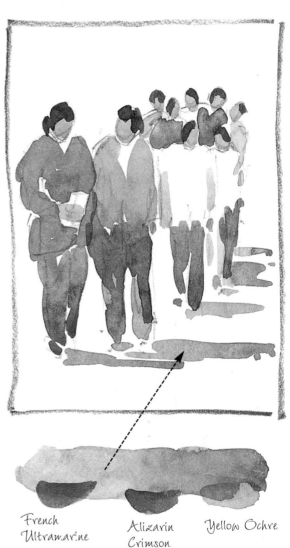

French Ultramarine   Alizarin Crimson   Yellow Ochre

3 *Continue painting in the figures. Notice how well the white areas of unpainted paper work for two of the figures.*

4 *Now paint the hair and see how the people come alive. Paint in the shadows on the ground to stop them from floating.*

SIMPLE BUILDINGS

A building without its details is just like the box you practiced painting earlier (page 22). Naturally, this is an oversimplification. But remember, if you can look at an object or scene and simplify it in your mind's eye before you start painting, you are well on your way to becoming a good artist.

Simplify

If you stood on a main street and were asked to paint it, it would naturally be too complicated for you. Before you can paint buildings, you must learn to simplify. Here are two very different but equally simple ways to get started.

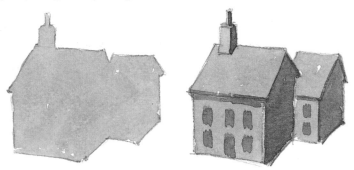

The house was a flat shape before the shadows were added. Remember, light against dark gives shape and form (page 22).

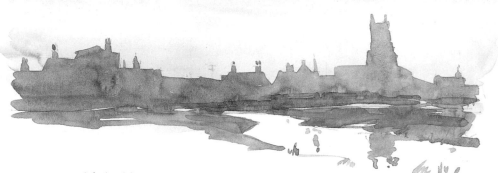

Another way to simplify buildings is to paint them in silhouette against a bright sky or sunset. Concentrate only on the outline form. I drew these buildings first, then painted the sky down and into the foreground. When it dried, I painted the buildings wet-on-wet, changing the colors very subtly as I worked (page 14).

Simple village

These village houses are all based on the simple box (page 22) and the yellow house opposite. It is light against dark that shows the form. I keep repeating this because it is very important. Look at the church tower in stage 1. It looks completely flat. Put a shadow on it, stage 2, and it becomes solid.

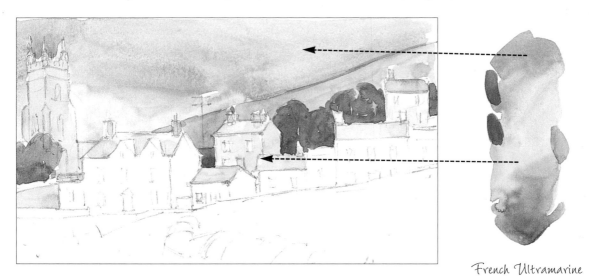

1 *Draw in with your 2B pencil. Paint in the background, leaving white paper for the white buildings. The painting looks flat, but notice how the yellow house stands out—light against the dark background.*

French Ultramarine
+ Alizarin Crimson
+ Yellow Ochre

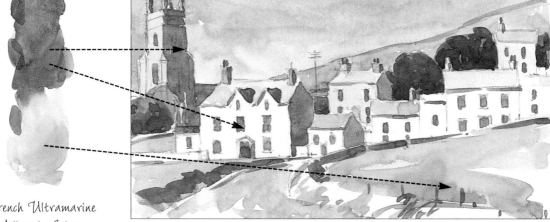

French Ultramarine
+ Alizarin Crimson
+ Yellow Ochre
+ Hooker's Green
+ Cadmium Yellow Light

2 *The sun is on the left, therefore the shadows are on the right. Paint them in, then paint the windows with the same color. They should just be square blobs of paint—no detail. Now paint the simple foreground.*

You can paint 79

EXERCISE Paint buildings

I have chosen this scene, made up from a real place with my own additions, to show how light against dark shows form and shape. Remember that to get crisp edges you must paint onto a dry surface; if the first layer of paint is still wet, your colors will merge and you will lose the shapes of the buildings.

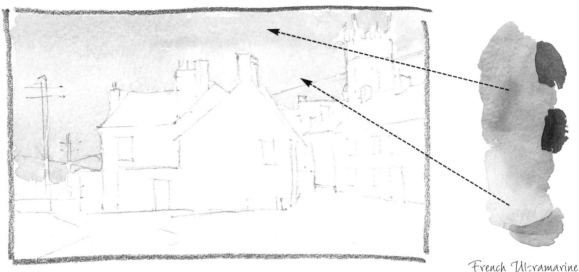

French Ultramarine
+ Alizarin Crimson
+ Yellow Ochre

1 *Draw in with your 2B pencil. Then paint the sky, working around the buildings. Use a graded color wash (page 13).*

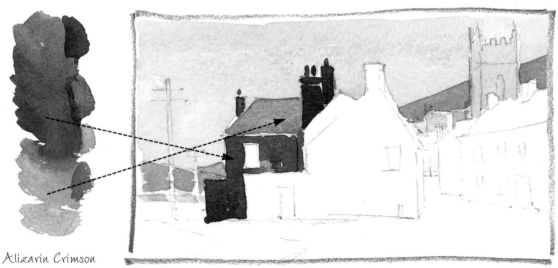

Alizarin Crimson
+ French Ultramarine
+ Yellow Ochre
+ Cadmium Red

2 *Paint the background hills, the church tower, and the dark house. It is important to get the silhouettes of the church and house right.*

The palette

French Ultramarine

Alizarin Crimson

Yellow Ochre

Cadmium Red

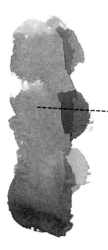

French Ultramarine
+ Alizarin Crimson
+ Yellow Ochre

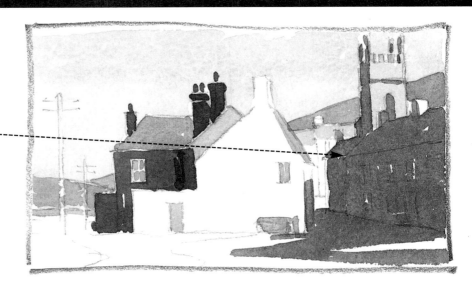

3 Use a wash to paint shadows (page 22) on the church tower, the row
 of houses, the road, and one side of the white house. Then paint the
windows and door.

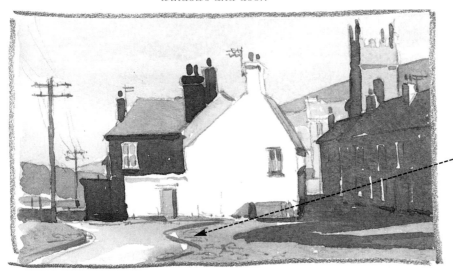

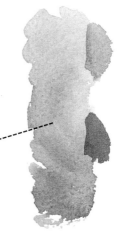

Yellow Ochre
+ Alizarin Crimson

4 Paint the foreground with a warm wash and go over the shadow.
 Finally, add a few dark accents wherever you feel they are needed.

You can paint 81

WATER

When water is painted well, it always looks good in a painting. The biggest trap that beginners fall into is to overwork water, making it look too complicated and unrealistic—and less "watery" with each brush stroke! The secret with water is to keep it simple.

Reflections

Look how simple this scene is. The water itself is unpainted paper; it is just the reflection that makes it appear to be water. It is important to put reflections in your water when possible.

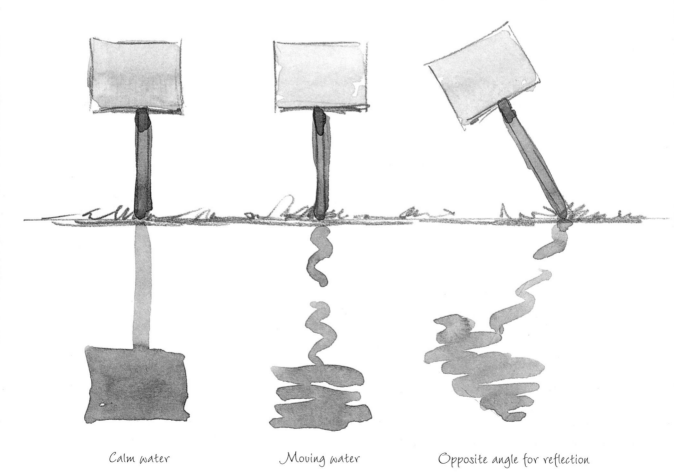

Calm water   Moving water   Opposite angle for reflection

Still water

If water is not moving, it reflects images like a mirror. But don't get too fussy about an exact image; you're making a painting, not a photographic copy.

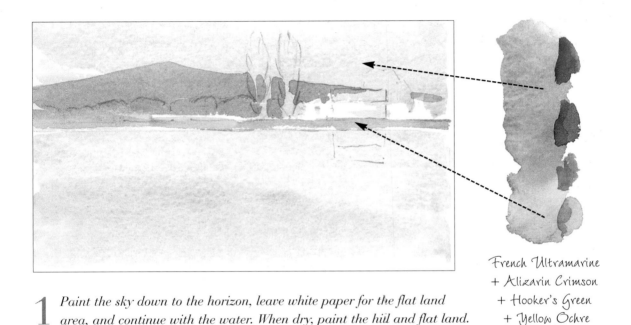

French Ultramarine
+ Alizarin Crimson
+ Hooker's Green
+ Yellow Ochre

1 *Paint the sky down to the horizon, leave white paper for the flat land area, and continue with the water. When dry, paint the hill and flat land.*

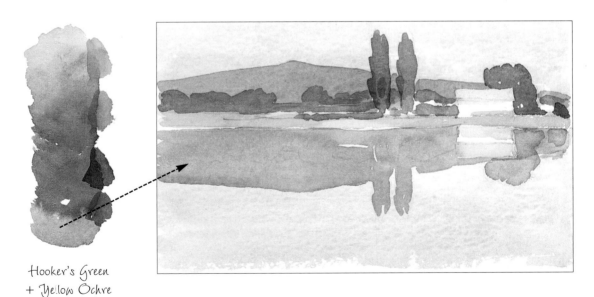

Hooker's Green
+ Yellow Ochre
+ Alizarin Crimson
+ French Ultramarine

2 *Finish the land, then paint in the reflections with one wash, starting with green and changing to gray. Remember, keep it simple; don't give in to the temptation to keep working on it.*

Moving water

Whether its motion is caused by a natural current, the wind, or boat traffic, moving water is easy to paint in watercolor and looks very effective.

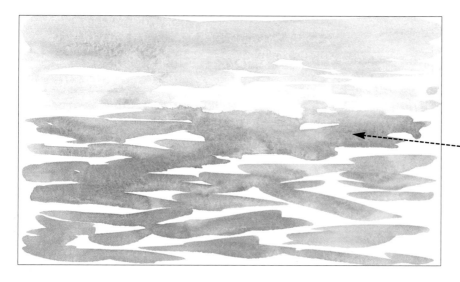

French Ultramarine
+ Alizarin Crimson
+ Yellow Ochre

1 *Using broken horizontal brush strokes, start at the top and work down. Leave areas of white paper to depict reflected light on the water.*

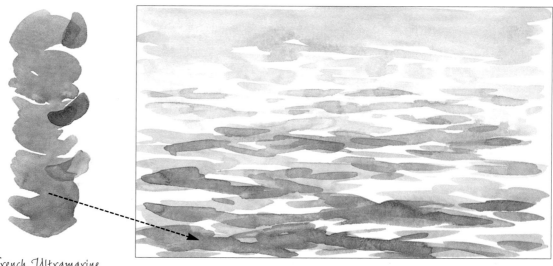

French Ultramarine
+ Alizarin Crimson
+ Yellow Ochre

2 *When the first stage is dry, paint over it with a darker color, still using broken horizontal brush strokes.*

Estuary water

There are no reflections from the land in this water. This often happens when the water is a long way off. But if you look closely, you can see reflections in the water from the sky. This is what helps the estuary look like water. Remember, the sky is always reflected in water.

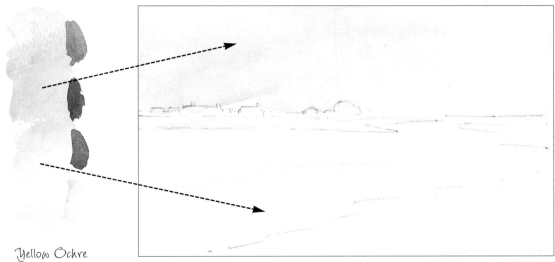

Yellow Ochre
+ Alizarin Crimson
+ French Ultramarine
+ Cadmium Yellow Light

1 *Paint in the sky and water with the same colors. Leave some white unpainted paper in the distant water. Paint in the land.*

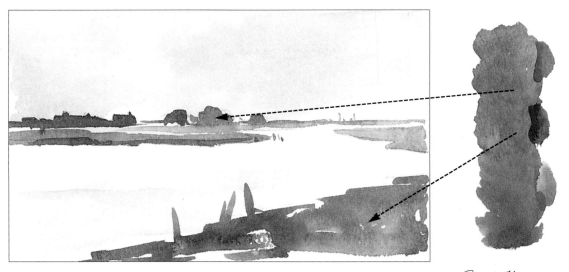

2 *Paint in the landscape. The time is evening, so it is in silhouette. Another reason the estuary appears to be water is that the dark land contrasts with the very light water.*

French Ultramarine
+ Alizarin Crimson
+ Yellow Ochre

Boats

If you spend some time painting scenes with water, at some point you will have to paint boats. You need to be reasonably good at drawing to tackle some boats, but there are ways of simplifying them. One method is to paint them in silhouette (see opposite). This takes away the need to include difficult detail.

1 *This boat has one wash painted over it. This is the technique that was used for the box on page 22.*

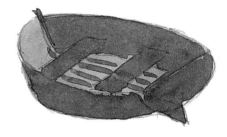

2 *Add the shadow with one wash and the boat becomes a solid, 3-D object and not a flat shape.*

1 *This small cruiser requires more drawing, but the shapes are simple. Observe them carefully; then paint the first wash. The two men give scale to the boat.*

2 *Paint the dark shadows, then the reflection. Now the boat looks as if it is in water.*

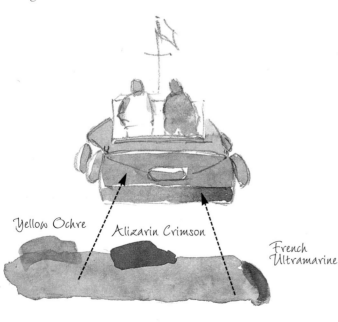

Yellow Ochre

Alizarin Crimson

French Ultramarine

Sketching boats

Take your sketchbook out and enjoy a day sketching boats. Don't draw or paint any in the foreground; draw them from a distance so that you lose most of the complicated detail. Detail will come automatically the more you practice.

Distant yacht
The white sail is the most important part of this sketch, because it is a recognizable image.

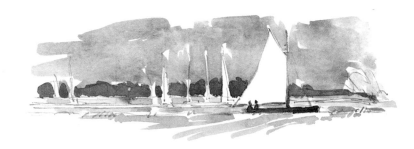

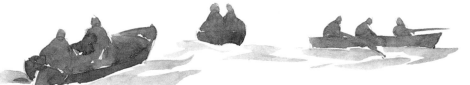

Silhouettes
Silhouettes are not an easy way to avoid learning to draw! But they are easier for a beginner to paint. Remember, a silhouette can be dark against light or light against dark.

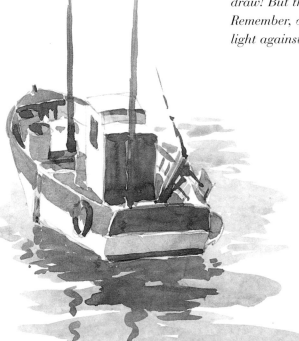

Fishing boat
This is the most adventurous sketch. You need to have drawing skills for this. But look how simple the boat image is, using light against dark to show form. And the reflection is also painted very simply.

EXERCISE Paint a boat

If you look at stage 4, this fishing boat looks complicated to paint. However. if you follow the stages carefully and you have been practicing, you won't have any problems. But first you must draw it carefully. Remember, the more you practice, the better you will get.

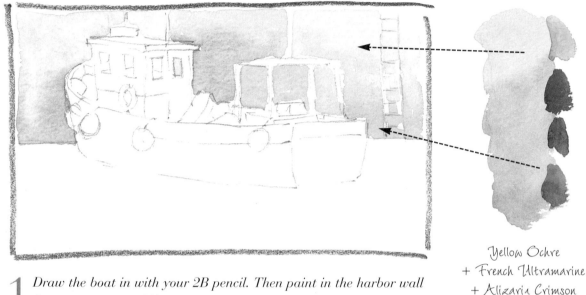

1 *Draw the boat in with your 2B pencil. Then paint in the harbor wall (wet-on-wet, page 14).*

Yellow Ochre + French Ultramarine + Alizarin Crimson + Hooker's Green

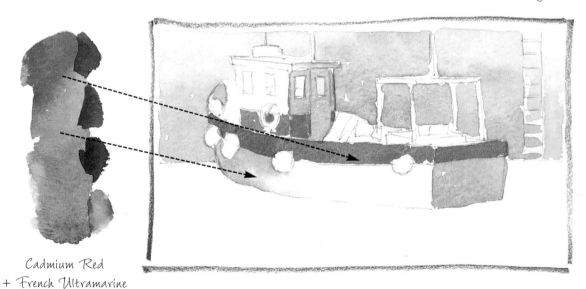

Cadmium Red + French Ultramarine + Alizarin Crimson + Yellow Ochre

2 *When the background is dry, paint the red color on the boat. When that dries, paint the shadow areas, going over the red when necessary.*

The palette

Yellow Ochre

French
Ultramarine

Alizarin Crimson

Hooker's Green

Cadmium Red

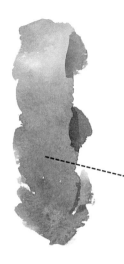

Hooker's Green
+ French Ultramarine
+ Yellow Ochre

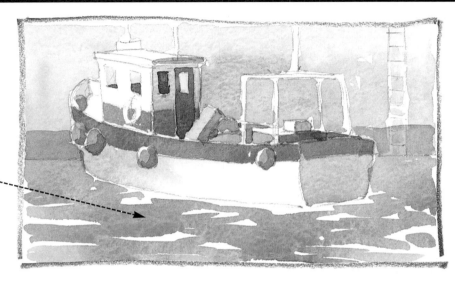

3 *Add more detail to to the boat, then paint in the water as you did for the exercise on page 84.*

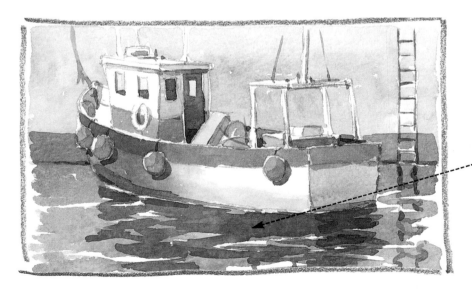

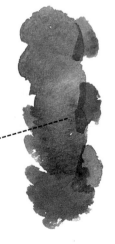

Hooker's Green
+ French Ultramarine
+ Alizarin Crimson

4 *Add some more darks and shadows to the boat. Paint in the ladder. Finally, paint in the reflections.*

Pebble beach

The coast is full of watercolor subjects. Because you can see the horizon, you get vast, uninterrupted skies to paint. But the obvious subjects are the beach and the ocean. Below is just one way of painting a pebble beach.

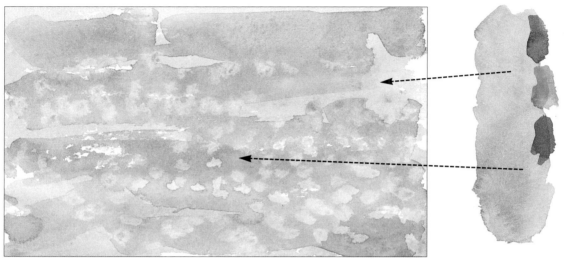

1 *Paint a wash, followed by another one with stronger colors. Then, with a tissue, lift out paint to represent pebbles (page 17).*

Alizarin Crimson
+ Yellow Ochre
+ French Ultramarine

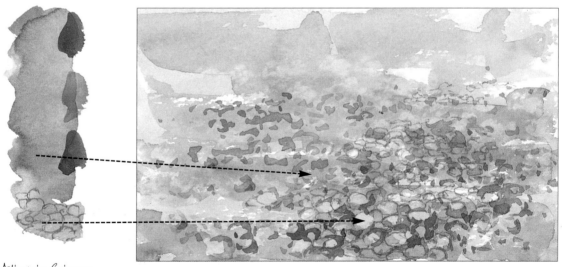

Alizarin Crimson
+ Yellow Ochre
+ French Ultramarine
+ Pencil

2 *With stronger color and shadow color, suggest the pebbles. Finish by drawing some pebble shapes with your 2B pencil over the dry paint.*

Waves

Waves are always moving and are therefore difficult to paint. It is helpful to sit and watch the patterns that they make until you become familiar with the shapes. You can also use photographs as a guide.

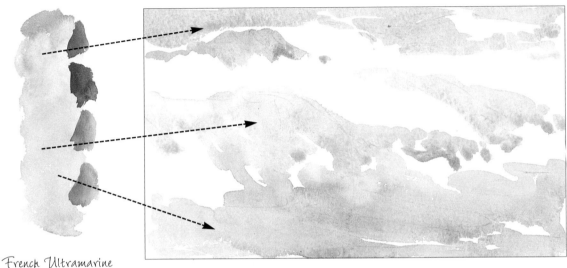

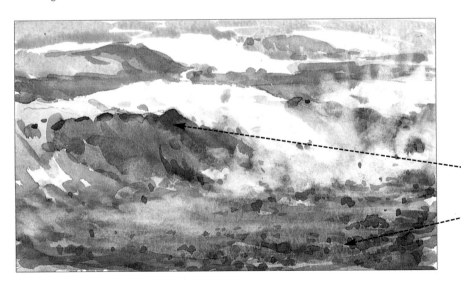

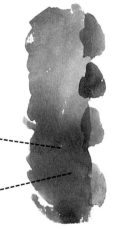

French Ultramarine
+ Alizarin Crimson
+ Hooker's Green
+ Yellow Ochre

1 *With a wet-on-wet wash (page 14), paint in the water, leaving white paper for the light-colored foam.*

2 *Using darker colors, paint under the breaking waves, then paint the beach. Now, with a wet brush, lift out areas to represent fine spray (page 17). Then add some dark brush strokes to represent thrown pebbles.*

French Ultramarine
+ Alizarin Crimson
+ Hooker's Green
+ Yellow Ochre

Sketching the coastline

Don't forget your sketchbook! There's always time and a variety of subjects to practice on, especially at the coast. Remember, sketches are a means of gathering information, and more importantly for a beginner, they are a way to make practicing enjoyable. It isn't the end result that matters; it's the fact that you have observed and drawn, gathering experience.

Deck chair
These are almost as difficult to sketch as to put up! This is a very well-known seaside image.

Pier
This is in silhouette, but you don't see detail if it is in the middle distance. Notice how simple the sea is.

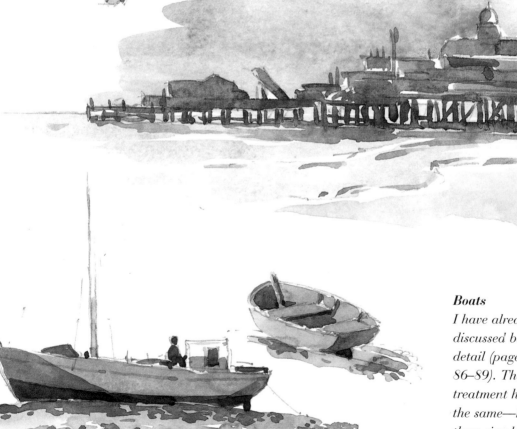

Boats
I have already discussed boats in detail (pages 86–89). The treatment here is the same—keep them simple.

Cliffs

Another traditional coastline view. Cliffs are simple to sketch, but very dramatic. Note how the people give scale.

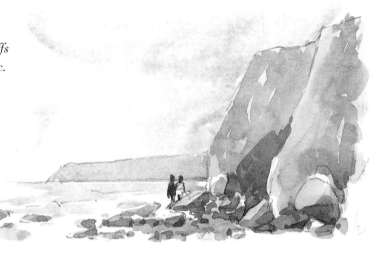

Crab

This is easy to draw, but more difficult to paint. The shell and claws were done wet-on-wet (page 14). When dry, another wash was applied to give crispness to the shell.

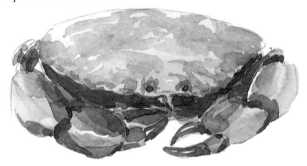

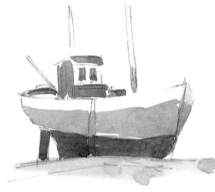

The red boat

This was painted very simply, using just two washes.

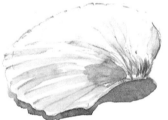

Shell

You can find these almost anywhere, and you can paint them on the beach or at home.

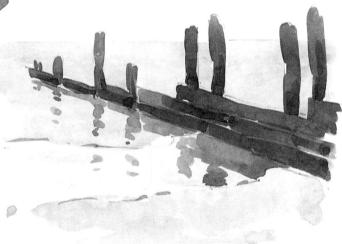

Windbreaks

This simple sketch works because the subject is uncomplicated and it is painted dark (posts) against light (water). Remember, silhouette shapes are very effective in watercolor.

DEMONSTRATION SEASCAPE

👀 AT A GLANCE...

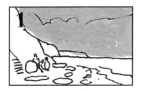
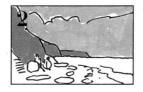
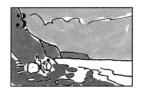
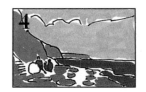

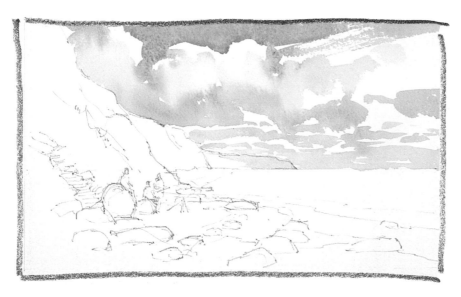

1 Draw in with your 2B pencil. With your big brush, paint in the blue sky. Then paint the clouds, letting the color merge with the blue sky in places. Leave some untouched edges to form crisp white clouds. Paint the distant clouds thinner.

2 Paint in the cliffs. Start with the distant ones in cool colors and work towards the nearest cliff, making the colors warmer as you go. Leave some white sunlit areas at the bottom of the distant cliffs and here and there on the foreground cliff.

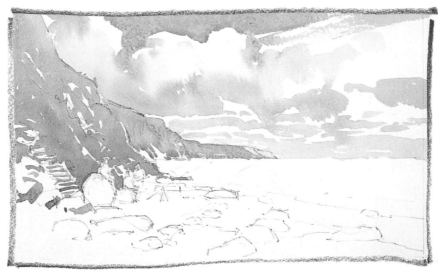

The palette

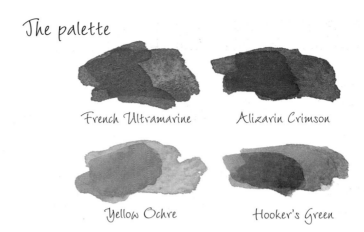

French Ultramarine

Alizarin Crimson

Yellow Ochre

Hooker's Green

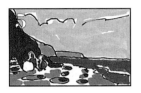

3 *Paint the beach using the same colors, but add more Yellow Ochre for the sand and pebbles. Paint the rocks freely, leaving small areas of white paper to represent water and sunlight on them.*

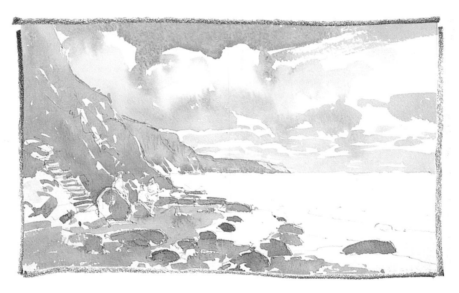

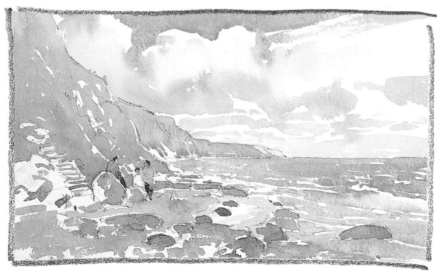

4 *With your small brush, paint the sea. Use Hooker's Green and French Ultramarine at the horizon, then continue using only the blue. Paint in horizontal brush strokes and leave white areas to represent waves. Then paint in the fishermen.*

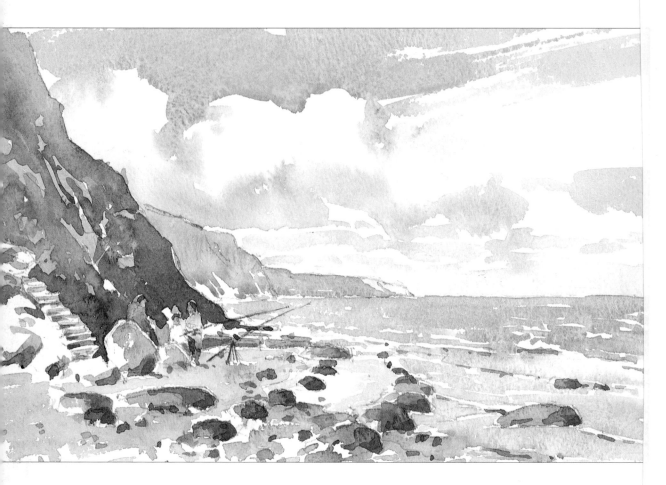

5 *Finished picture: watercolor paper, 7½ x 12 in. Now comes the part that brings the foreground towards you and moves the distant cliffs away from you. Paint a dark wash on the foreground cliff, changing the colors as you work (wet-on-wet, page 14). Put dark shadows on the rocks. Finally, paint in the fishing rods.*

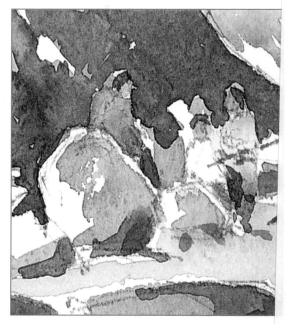

Detail: *This is the most important part of the painting. The contrast between the dark cliff and the distant light cliffs creates distance, and the fishermen add life and mystery—what are they talking about?*